Imagining Politics

Imagining Politics critically examines two interpretations of government. The first comes from popular culture fictions about politics, the second from academic political science. Stephen Benedict Dyson argues that fictions and theories both function as attempts at meaning making—making sensible the otherwise insensible realm of political behavior.

By taking fiction seriously, and by arguing that political science theory is homologous to fiction, the book offers a fresh perspective on both. The specialist is challenged to think anew not just about fictions such as *The West Wing, House of Cards, Borgen, Black Mirror,* and *Scandal,* but also about the assumptions that construct the discipline of political science itself.

Imagining Politics is also about our political moment. The two populist shocks of our time—Brexit and the election of Trump—are new context here. Dyson traces how Trump and the Brexite paigned against our image of politics as usual, and won.

Stephen Benedict Dyson is Professor of Political Science at the sity of Connecticut.

Imagining Politics

Interpretations in Political Science and Political Television

Stephen Benedict Dyson

UNIVERSITY OF MICHIGAN PRESS | ANN ARBOR

Published in the United States of America by
the University of Michigan Press

First published July 2019

A CIP catalog record for this book is available from the British Library.

ISBN 978-0-472-07424-2 (hardcover)
ISBN 978-0-472-05424-4 (paper)
ISBN 978-0-472-12588-3 (ebook)

I dedicate this book to Rosa Emilia, with love.

Contents

Digital materials related to this title can be found on the Fulcrum platform via the following citable URL: https://doi.org/10.3998/mpub.10191802

Acknowledgments

How do we make sense of politics? This book looks at two ways of making political meaning: (1) academic theories of political science and (2) fictional televised portrayals of how government works. I argue that the two have surprising similarities. Both political science theories and televised political fictions are based on assumptions about politics, directing our attention to some things and away from others, telling some stories but not others. By setting these two sources in dialogue, our images of politics are revealed, and we expose a central way in which our society thinks about itself.

I have had some valuable help in writing this book. My lively colleagues Alexander Anievas, Fred Lee, and Tom Hayes read drafts of the manuscript and gave excellent feedback. Tom and another valued colleague, Prakash Kashwan, accompanied me to the Trump rally described in the book. That was an experience. Jeff Dudas went above and beyond, providing extensive written feedback and moderating a workshop on the draft manuscript. Students in my "Screen Politics" seminar worked with an earlier version of the text and helped me sharpen its arguments. My mum and dad, as has been the case with each of my books, dove into the text and offered plentiful commentary ranging from line edits to critiques of the whole argument. Reviewers for the press offered many good suggestions, and I hope they are pleased with the changes I made in response.

Elizabeth Demers at the University of Michigan Press saw the project through from proposal to completion. I am grateful for her staunch support of what is a somewhat unconventional work. John Sides at the Monkey Cage, a political science site hosted by the *Washington Post*, published related essays of mine as I dove deeper into the topic of politics and popular culture. I am similarly grateful for his support of this unusual angle on political science.

1 | Imagining Politics

Senator Richard Monckton, candidate for the presidency of the United States of America, climbs out of his black sedan and glowers. He could greet the voters in the crowd in front of him, but instead he stands stock-still. Shoulders hunched. Eyes narrow and dark. Suddenly journalists and cameramen flood the scene, and Monckton is alive. A smile erupts across his face. He plunges into the crowd, slapping hands and grabbing arms. "Yeah! Yeah! Yeah!" The crowd surges, the flashbulbs explode again and again. "Good to see you! Yeah!" At the doorway of his office building, he gives a sweeping wave to the crowd. "Yeah!"

Once he is inside the building, his arms quickly return to his sides. His shoulders resume their hunch. His eyes become narrow once more. He is locked in a struggle for power in Washington, DC. The retiring president is plotting to steal the election from Monckton. The CIA director is being blackmailed by the president. The FBI is involved. It is a deep-state conspiracy, hidden from public view.

Monckton is the fictional protagonist of the television miniseries *Washington Behind Closed Doors* (1977), which was inspired by Richard Nixon's years in office. It was based on the book *The Company* by Nixon hand John Ehrlichman, who tried to make sense of his experiences in Washington by writing a work of fiction. The details were made up, but the deeper truths—the malevolence, the infighting, the venality of the political elite—were authentic. The show reflected a new cultural disillusionment with a political class that had brought about Vietnam and Watergate. Transmitted through the now ubiquitous medium of television, *Washington Behind Closed Doors* reflected and reinforced new anxieties about American government.

At the same time that television executives green-lit this ominous interpretation of American politics, political scientists were also trying to make sense of the era. Most had abandoned the belief that careful analysis of the Constitution was all that was required to understand politics. The hopeful verities of mid-century—that a liberal consensus reigned in an empire of reason—were less and less persuasive. Instead, political scientists now argued, politicians must be seen for what they are rather than what we wished them to be: self-interested actors getting away with anything they could.[1] The new theory of government was that it was an insider game rather than a transparent and virtuous public square.

This book is about politics in our imaginations as they are guided by televised fictions and the academic discipline of political science. Its argument is that political fictions and political science speak to the historical and cultural moment that produces them, reflecting and shaping the beliefs and anxieties of their time and place. They speak to each other too. They are structures of interpretation that paint pictures of our politics.

From the sophisticated way my students have engaged with earlier versions of this argument, it is clear that they already know that television shows are meaningful sites of cultural conversation. Some of my scholarly colleagues, though, might think these fictions are nothing more than entertainment.[2] It seems wise to begin, then, with a few words about the genesis of the book and the scope and limits of its argument.

Imagining Politics contends that political science theories and televised political fictions are both interpretations of government. As we will see in the chapters to come, these dual interpretations—one seeking the status of scientific objectivity, the other demurring that it is just telling stories—imagine politics to be about self-interested elites pursuing and using power.

This image—politics as a game played among the elite in pursuit of power—is useful to fictioneers and social scientists alike. For screenwriters it affords significant storytelling possibilities. Compelling narratives begin with a character who wants something and an obstacle to their getting it.[3] The pursuit of power in an intra-elite game satisfies these dramatic requirements. Politics can make for good TV. For political scientists this image of politics isolates a few key players and suggests they behave in predictable ways: as rational actors driven by self-interested calculations. In this manner the fluid and inchoate activity of politics can be organized into a form that is amenable to systematic study.

The simple contention of this book is that these images must be judged by how useful they are in making sense of the political world, and how connected to or alienated from our government they make us feel. They are interpretations of the phenomenon of politics that seek to explain or to entertain, directing our attention toward some things and away from others, telling a story to help us make sense of an otherwise insensible realm of activity. They constitute plausible—perhaps even the most plausible—

interpretations of government. But as interpretations, they do not reflect in a value-free way the phenomena they address, nor do they exhaust the possibility of alternate interpretations.[4]

Why would I write this book? And as a political scientist, should I be watching quite this much television? *Imagining Politics* is the extension of a line of reasoning I began in my previous book, *Otherworldly Politics*. There I engaged the genre of speculative fiction, tracing the connections between images of human behavior in science fiction and fantasy and the theorizing of international relations (IR) scholars. I found that the key question was the same for both: imagine a world that works like *this*— what happens in that world?

I believe that works about US and comparative politics can similarly by read as acts of imagination and thereby set in dialogue with political fictions. Still, I hesitated on whether to pursue this project. Perhaps one book about political fictions was enough, and I should get back to reality. Then Trump happened. In the summer of 2016, I stood in a sweltering hall in Fairfield, Connecticut, watching the Republican presidential candidate. Mr. Trump was famous from television, specifically from the genre of reality television, that odd fusion of cinema verité and fake spontaneity.

I reflected upon this man who seemed to have jumped genres from business to television to politics, like a crossover TV episode where characters from one show make a guest appearance on another. I watched over the course of his campaign as he acted in ways that were entirely out of the ordinary for presidential candidates and entirely against the expectations of political scientists. No pivot to the ideological center for him. No apology for one scandal after another. No focus-grouped appeals to swing voters. No blitzing the airwaves with paid television advertisements. The political class of journalists and social scientists and consultants and strategists didn't know how to interpret Trump. GOP leaders—and, later, Democrats too—didn't know how to stop him.

I remembered the people in the crowd around me, in "Make America Great Again" baseball caps and "Hillary for Prison" shirts, rapt as Trump talked of the average Americans who had been ignored and manipulated by the media elite, the political elite, and the academics on campus.

As I show in the coming chapters, our fiction and our social science had for decades portrayed politics as an insider game played by self-interested elites. Trump ran against this dominant conception of politics, and he won.[5] So *Imagining Politics*, in one reading, is the story of how a web of meaning about government was built, through multiple iterations of television shows and academic theories, and how these meanings collapsed, for a time at least, and left us wondering what had happened. That is how to read this book as an argument about contemporary politics, with each chapter adding bits to the image of politics coming from fictions like *The West Wing, Scandal,* and *Yes, Minister* and coming from political science theories like ambition theory, median voter theory, and the unilateral presidency.

The book can also be read as a work of method: an argument about the seriousness of fiction and its homologous function to social science theory. Political fictions and political science speak of and speak to the historical and cultural moment that produces them. They reflect and shape the beliefs and anxieties of their time and place. They speak to each other too. They tell stories about the actions, the goals, and the competence of our leaders.

Some limits to the argument: I do not claim to know whether the disruption of political meaning brought about by Trump (and the ideas and movement he represents) is temporary or permanent. Further, I am certainly not arguing against the use of the scientific method or the rational choice assumptions of mainstream US political science. I see these assumptions as neither pathological nor tragic—two terms that have been used by their critics.[6] My contention is that they are useful fictions, not more, not less. If I did not have admiration for the classics of political science addressed in the chapters to come, I would not have engaged with them at all; indeed, most scholars who write about politics and popular culture simply ignore mainstream work rather than seek to engage it in a dialogue, as I do here. My argument is not that the scientific-rational approach in political science is "wrong"; in fact, it may be more "right" than any other interpretation. My point is just that: the scientific-rational approach of US political science is an interpretation rather than a scientific truth. Questions of right or wrong are subordinate to the deeper issue of what meaning is made by an interpretation and what the consequences of those meanings are.

Finally, I have attempted to maintain a balance in this book between accessibility and sophistication. There may be points—hopefully not too many—at which a specialist feels that that a cutting-edge theory is not covered in depth, or a nonspecialist finds that a piece of jargon has been used where something more straightforward would have done the job. I have aimed to accurately engage academic concepts and ideas while keeping the terminology to a minimum and the book moving along. There are many kinds of students of politics, from the college undergraduate, to the professor, to the engaged citizen outside of the university. Perhaps I am overly ambitious, but I would like the book to have something to say to each of these audiences.

There are two necessary tasks for the rest of this chapter. First we must think about the underpinnings of the argument that television can be taken seriously. Then we must think about whether it is reasonable to regard theories of political science as imaginative interpretations. If these two tasks can be accomplished, then we have a foundation for the rest of the book: a dialogue between imaginings of politics in television fiction and social science theory.

Some Principles for Taking Television Seriously

Here are four principles that underpin the argument that television can be taken seriously.[7] The first is that television can be more than entertainment. Television reflects, constructs, and perpetuates how society thinks and talks about itself.[8] In this line of reasoning, the social world is one of negotiated meanings that humans work out with one another through continual conversation, including via mass media. Meanings are attached to political things—people, rules, and institutions—through the development of shared mental constructs. These shared mental constructs are the stuff of a society's discourse.[9]

Culture is the broad term for those activities by which meaning is generated, circulated, and perpetuated. Popular culture is, by definition, the form of culture to which most people are exposed most often. Television is a central element of popular culture. Therefore, storytelling on television is one way that a society makes sense of itself.[10]

The second principle for taking television seriously is that the meanings in television must be recovered and interpreted by methods other than the counting and tallying of, for instance, how many people watch a program or what proportion of time is devoted in a news broadcast to one point of view.[11] Counting and tallying is crucial; polemics that pit counting approaches against deep reading approaches tend to be reductive. But television programs rely on cultural knowledge structures to give meaning to their plots, actors, and aesthetic choices, and recognizing this interplay requires an interpretive approach. Such an approach suggests that culture is written into television programs by producers and is read out of them by audiences. In this way, television circulates and perpetuates meaning.[12]

This point was brilliantly made by a central figure in the development of television studies, the cultural theorist Stuart Hall.[13] By the late 1960s,

Hall noted, television had supplanted radio as the dominant form of electronic media. The US government, concerned about the impact of this new and seemingly hypnotic medium, commissioned a large-scale study of its effect on children.[14] The hypothesis of the study was that violence shown on TV led to violence in real life. The methodology was counting and tallying: each program was watched by a researcher with a notepad, who would tally up every violent episode shown. Children who watched varying amounts of TV were then monitored for violent behavior. The study found plenty of violence on TV but no clear link between watching TV and acting in a violent manner.

Hall posited that no link was found because television did not transmit meaning by simply showing actions on-screen a certain number of times. Instead, images on television were encoded with meaning based on context, and viewers decoded these meanings based on cultural knowledge structures that turned sequences of acts into stories with messages. Hall found that the most violent genre of television was the Western. Yet much of the violence in Westerns was committed by lawmen against outlaws. The lawmen were cool, competent, and altruistic. This message—the ideal of chivalric professionalism and justice rather than the imperative to commit imitative acts of violence—was the one audiences read. "How many other, crucial kinds of meaning were in fact transmitted whilst researchers were busy counting the bodies?" Hall asked.[15]

The third principle, then, is that television programming offers a complex amalgam of messages and cultural information, with the person, thing, or act on-screen given meaning only by the shared mental constructs that place the person, thing, or act within a societal conversation. Like a novel or a film, a television program must be regarded as a text into which are written codes and meanings and that is read by audiences drawing upon cultural knowledge structures. Audiences might or might not read the text the way the authors intend them to. And different audiences may read the same text differently. Meaning, then, must be recovered by the researcher through analysis of the conversations that inhabit and surround the text. Simply put, texts have subtexts and exist in contexts. They also have relationships among one another; they quote and modify, accrete and subvert. Texts have this quality of "intertextuality." In Mikhail Bakhtin's famous formulation, the text "tastes of the contexts in which it has lived its socially charged life."[16]

The final principle behind taking television seriously is this: the things society talks about in its popular culture are often the central issues of its life. These are inherently political questions of power relations: who has it, and how should it be used? In this book the popular culture that is addressed—televised political fictions—is explicitly about political power. But the popular culture/politics nexus goes well beyond the genre of political fictions, as television deals almost constantly in encoded images of, for example, class, gender, race, and ethics.[17]

Some Principles for Regarding Political Science as a Set of Imaginative Interpretations

If television is not just entertainment, what is the argument that political science is not just the direct observation, recording, and explanation of reality? How can I argue that political science deals in interpretations, rather than factual recitations of immutable truths? Here are three principles that underpin the argument that works of political science can be regarded as imaginative interpretations and thus set in conversation with political fictions.[18]

First, the scope of activities we regard as political are simply too vast and too ambiguous to record and report in totality, at least in a way that will lead to significant understanding. An attempt to avoid imagination by simply recording facts and figures cannot succeed. Thus, scientists of all kinds build models of reality, abstracting from the noise of their realm of study those signal features that drive actions and outcomes. These models rely upon theories, which are creative insights into the operation of a part of the world. These theories—these creative insights—ask what features of a realm of activity matter, how do we know them when we see them, and how do they relate to one another?

The image of politics held by a political scientist is, then, a model rather than a mirror of reality.[19] In this sense it is homologous (it performs the same function) to the modeling of politics behind televised fictions. Decisions are made in both mediums about what is to be focused upon, what is to be ignored, and about how the things that are focused upon relate to one another. The criteria are different—the social scientist is looking for the best explanation, and the fictioneer for the best entertainment—but the essential imaginative act is, if not the same, at least related in purpose.

Political scientists require, then, coherent and shared models of politics that provide plausible accounts of why and how political activity proceeds as it does.[20] These models, and the conceptual vocabularies that accompany them, are the language by which political scientists talk to one another. They are perpetuated via the communicative technologies of the discipline, which are its academic journals and conferences. And they are transmitted to a wider audience—that is, students—via the university classroom.

The second principle, then, is that political science, like all professionalized academic disciplines, is a community of persons holding shared images of their subject designed to (1) offer a plausible set of explanations for the phenomena of interest and (2) extend and perpetuate these images through the production of new research and the transmission of the results of this research to others.[21]

The final principle is that a large discipline like political science can contain within it a variety of images of politics. These subdisciplinary communities have their own vocabularies and concepts. In this book we are most interested in an image of politics that developed in the United States and is associated with the study of American and comparative government. This genre of work is committed to a philosophy of explanation known as the scientific method, and to an interpretation of political action known as rational choice theory.[22]

Detailed explanation of the assumptions underlying these works comes in the relevant chapters, but we can say a few words here about the genre as a whole. The scientific approach, as applied to politics, imagines the political world as a set of separate parts and pieces that relate to one another as the causes and effects of behaviors.[23] These relationships, wherein a change (say, in magnitude) of one part leads to a change (again in magnitude) of another, are posited to operate consistently across time and space and to do so in a manner that leaves behind perceptible evidence that can be cataloged by researchers. These researchers are guided by assumptions that direct attention toward what evidence should be gathered and what it means.

This image came to the fore in the United States after the Second World War and was known as *behavioralism*.[24] As implied by the name, the core assumption was that the observed behavior of the politician and the voter must be at the center of scientific accounts of politics. Behavior was a matter of fact, not of virtue, ethics, or high hopes. The Constitution of the United States, for example, offered a nice story about how politics should operate, but the proper concern of the political scientist was what political actors did, not what the founding texts of the nation said they should do.

In the classic works examined in this book, behavioralist approaches are often paired with a postulate of rationality.[25] The rational choice school of thought, which swept into political science beginning in the 1960s and 1970s, posited that political actors wanted to maximize their utility—a fungible concept that could be defined as a policy or political good (for example, share of the vote). The rational politician pursued this goal single-mindedly, was able to accurately calculate which actions would lead to the greatest amount of this good, and invariably took the action with the biggest payoff.[26]

Rational choice approaches not only provided a powerful way to organize and interpret the data generated by the behavioralists' cataloging of political phenomena but also creatively linked observed cause to observed effect by positing that the intervening mechanism—the political actor—responds to stimuli through a calculation of what is best for them. This calculation is imagined to be universal; all actors given the same incentives make the same choices. The majority of the classic works of political science addressed in this book take these two principles—that politics is best studied through the scientific method and that political behavior should be understood as the rational pursuit of interests—as axiomatic. They therefore form one genre of political science, which is set in dialogue in the chapters to come with the genre of televised political fictions.

Outline of the Book

The rest of the book explores these conversations by pairing in each chapter a televised political fiction with classic work in political science where both are addressing the same subject; for example, the American presidency. The pairs limn images of politics that together constitute a vocabulary that has defined how we think and talk about the nature of our government.[27]

The chapters contain a reading of a televised fiction, an account of classic work in political science, and the real-world politics implicated by both. At various points the focus shifts among the three. At some points the focus is on how science and fiction coalesce around a shared interpretation of politics; at some points how science and fiction offer interpretations that are at odds with one another; and at still other points on how an interpretation directly influenced, or was influenced by, specific political acts.

Thus in chapter 2, Richard E. Neustadt's theory of presidential power is paired with the Aaron Sorkin fiction *The West Wing*. Neustadt and Sorkin advance a conception of politics centered on small groups of the exceptionally able. These elites act as patriarchs to the benighted land over which they preside. Yet they are under siege, armed with little more than a felicitous turn of phrase.

Chapter 3 offers a second image of the American presidency in fiction and political science. *House of Cards* shows a hyperrational chief executive exercising the formal powers of the office to the maximum. This fictional representation is mirrored in political science by studies of the president as a "unilateral rational actor"—a line of work that supplanted Neustadt's more humanistic court politics interpretation. Yet *House of Cards* also draws on cultural resources beyond political science, such as Shakespeare, and proximate real-world analogies, such as the career of Lyndon B. Johnson. In one sense this fiction bolsters the political science view of elites as driven by ambition, little more than guided missiles locking onto the highest office they can achieve. In a second reading, *House of Cards* acts to question this interpretation, implicating rival contextual and psychodynamic understandings of political action.

Chapter 4 addresses the boundary between private and public life, tightly drawn by scientific-rational conceptions of politics but thrown into question by the political fiction *Scandal*. Shonda Rhimes's kinetic melodrama interprets politics via private flaws. In her world everyone in public life is guilty of unconscionable personal behavior. The show's popular appeal rests on voyeurism. I pair this televised fiction with political science work that makes meaning of elite malfeasance by conceiving of it as rational advantage seeking.

Chapter 5 travels outside of the US context. The Danish political fiction *Borgen* interprets politics as compromise. Some political scientists believe it is the rules of the electoral system that shape the possibilities for political compromise. Denmark, with its proportional representation system and large number of political parties, seems to be a paradigmatic example of these forces in action. However, compromise has a cultural aspect too. Danish institutions are the result of unique historical experience and are actuated by a set of norms and meanings in addition to rules and calculations. And in this fiction, Prime Minister Birgitte Nyborg navigates her own compromise between public and private obligations.

Chapter 6 and chapter 7 address two British fictions: the satire of bureaucracy in *Yes, Minister* and the satire of spin in *The Thick of It*. *Yes, Minister* took the scientific-rational view of politics and made it into a perfectly realized farce. Public choice theory, a movement popular with conservative thinkers in the 1960s and 1970s, argued that neither politicians nor bureaucrats act in the public interest but are instead at war with each other, behind closed doors, in pursuit of their private interests. The results are frequently absurd. Politicians are often bemused and defeated by savvy bureaucrats. This was a view of governance brought to the screen in the shape of the harried politician Jim Hacker and Sir Humphrey, an elegant and scheming mandarin.

A generation of the UK political elite grew up watching *Yes, Minister*, among them almost all of the politicians who would form Tony Blair's Labour governments of the 1990s and early 2000s. They came into office determined not to be subordinate to the permanent bureaucracy. They marginalized the civil service and relied on special advisers, a set of political and media operatives who emphasized message discipline. The clashes that resulted between staid bureaucrats and macho special advisers were at the heart of *The Thick of It*, a farce about the frantic, self-defeating efforts of politicos to project an image of control. More than this, the absurdist *Thick of It* portrays a politics on the precipice: an unsustainable and hollow technocracy populated by experts in self-advancement who have become disconnected from the people they were supposed to represent.

In chapter 8 a bundle of meaning is assembled to try to understand two era-defining events: (1) the British vote to leave the European Union and (2) the victory of Donald J. Trump in the 2016 US presidential election. These two events were rejections of the discourse of the political elite. Both were driven by characters who would be out of place in our standard political fictions. I make meaning of this new form of politics as populism and argue that for interpretive leverage we must look to unusual fictions. Brexit and Trump are interpreted through the British techno-dystopia series *Black Mirror* and the US reality television show *The Apprentice*.

It is, though, to our first pairing of fiction and political science theory that we now turn: an examination of the American presidency through the eyes of Aaron Sorkin, creator of *The West Wing*, and Richard Neustadt, author of the political science classic *Presidential Power*.

2 | Persuasion—*The West Wing*

"What have I done wrong?" Richard E. Neustadt, political scientist and adviser to presidents, asked toward the end of his life. He had written a classic study of the American presidency, yet he felt rejected by an academic discipline he felt was far removed from the realities of government. He could not reconcile himself to how some political scientists had misunderstood his book *Presidential Power and the Modern Presidents*. He felt that his colleagues had not grasped its arguments about the subtle and personal influence of presidents, had not appreciated its lovingly crafted stories, almost fables, about the presidential struggle to exert influence over national affairs.

"Nobody noticed . . . what the book was about," he said. "I don't feel that it was a great success." At the start of his academic career in the late 1950s, he already believed political science was "a boring subject." He thought the discipline had only deteriorated in the decades since, overly consumed with scientific technique over real-world substance.[1]

In Washington, DC's National Cathedral, President Josiah "Jed" Bartlet is at the funeral of his oldest confidant, a woman he has known since his schooldays. Dolores Landingham, secretary to the president of the United States, bought her first new car at the age most people retire, then was hit by a drunk driver on her way home from the dealership.[2] At the end of the memorial service, the president, a devout Catholic, asks to be left alone inside the cathedral. He walks toward the pulpit and then stops, raises his chin, and says, "You're a son of a bitch."

When she first met him at his exclusive New England prep school, Mrs. Landingham had called young Jed a "boy king . . . a foot smarter than the other boys in the class. You're blessed with inspiration. You must have sensed it by now." A boy king then. A president now. Yet powerless before God. And angry too.

"You're a son of a bitch. You feckless thug." Bartlet has struggled as president against political opposition, natural disaster, his own multiple sclerosis. He has lied about his illness, sullied his self-image as a pure and honest politician. He has wrestled with a globalized economy to create 3.8 million new jobs. Bailed out Mexico. Increased foreign trade. Set aside tens of millions of acres of land for conservation. "We're not fighting a war. I've raised three children." That's not enough? *"Cruciatus in crucem! Eas in Crucem!"* To hell with your punishments! To hell with you!

This chapter recovers, from Neustadt and from *The West Wing*, an image of politics as intra-elite *persuasion*. Politics is interpreted in these texts as contingent and human, about relationships and perceptions, skill and knowledge. The personal qualities of the president—be it Jed Bartlet of *The West Wing* or the FDR-Truman-Eisenhower comparisons in Richard Neustadt's *Presidential Power*—are the crucial determinants of political success or failure. Presidents must deploy rhetoric, insight, knowledge, and bravery in seeking to convince those in other parts of the political elite to take action. Advisers to the president are important in helping him, but ultimately the responsibility rests with the person in the Oval Office.

The presidency as depicted in *Presidential Power* and *The West Wing* is weak. It is a place for people of high learning and good motives marooned in a country where these qualities are in short supply. This is a satisfying image of politics for the political and academic elite and the upscale audience of *The West Wing*. They imagine themselves besieged in their palaces of words and learning, surrounded by barbarians whom they must pacify and reform.

Reading *The West Wing* through Neustadt, and vice versa, produces this interpretation of politics as intra-elite persuasion amid the benighted masses. I situate both texts, Neustadt's and Sorkin's, in the time and place from which they came and excavate the discourses they contain. In situating *Presidential Power*, particular attention is paid to Neustadt's personal experiences as an adviser to US presidents and to a specific moment in the development of modern political science when the hunger was for studies of how politics works in practice rather than on paper. Neustadt, though, would end his career frustrated that his studies of triumph and foible in the nation's highest office were denigrated by what he saw as an increasingly mathematically inclined discipline. In political fiction, by contrast, Neustadt's image of the presidency lives on. It bursts out of *The West Wing*, about a gifted rhetorician and paternal humanist overwhelmed by the demands of his office and the disappointing capacities of the people he leads.

Persuasion

Neustadt's subject was presidential power, but his theme was presidential weakness. As an adviser to Harry S. Truman and John F. Kennedy, he had seen firsthand the gap between constitutional authority and practical influence. The president only *appears* to be atop the political system, Neustadt concluded. The real struggle is to be on top "in fact as well as in name."[3]

Neustadt saw the presidency as the underpowered engine of the political system. Effective government depends on actions that only the president can take. Yet few in the wider political system are required to do his bidding in return. Neustadt interpreted the presidency as a clerkship, not a dictatorship. So many issues and events press upon the president that discharging even the minimum of his responsibilities is a monumental achievement. When he wants to advance his agenda, the president begins as if in a wind tunnel, fighting for each small step forward and in constant danger of being blown off his feet.

"Is the presidency possible?" Neustadt asked, watching Jimmy Carter trying to gain control.[4] Most of the episodes he recounted in *Presidential Power* were variations on a theme, "the story of a failure." Most of the time, presidents are responding to crises. That is "what presidents do first."[5]

Presidents are weak, Neustadt thought, but not necessarily doomed. Self-help is their only route to success; they must understand the nature of their power and guard it jealously. Only they can do it. No one else, even their closest advisers, experiences the precise mixture of perspective and obligation that they do. They must be politicians, not heroes. Franklin D. Roosevelt, a master of tactics and strategy, was the right model for a president. Dwight D. Eisenhower, whom Neustadt disdained as a "hero seeking national unity," was too passive.[6] He let his power atrophy.

The president's task is to translate the incoherence of the office into a coherent projection of authority. The disparate and confusing responsibilities and vantage points of the presidency must be spun into a convincing portrait of a person in charge. This portrait must be shown to the other actors in the political system, fooling them into thinking they must do what the president wants.

The statutory powers of the presidency—bits and pieces of formal authority in the shape of executive orders and other commands—are not dispositive. If used intelligently and supplemented with bluffing and other manipulative arts, they can be useful. But if the president has to resort to formal powers to achieve his goals, that means that other, better ways have failed.[7]

The first resort of the presidency should be persuasion, not command. The Congress, the states, the courts, the media, must be convinced to do the president's bidding because they see it as in their own interest to do so.

If the president has to act without them, or try to compel them, then he has already lost.

The president must seem to have benefits to give to others or threaten to take away. This requires of the president a steady dose of impression management as he faces the rest of the political elite. He must loom large in their minds as a skillful and resolute bargainer. They must fear the consequences of defying him and believe he is strong and consistent enough to keep his side of any deal.[8]

Presidents must make choices with an eye to enhancing, or at least protecting, their future influence. The future looms over the present as the expectation that the president will be strong tomorrow compels others in the elite to give him what he wants today. When a president looks weak today, the assumption is that he will be weak tomorrow as well, so there is little to fear in defying him.

He must be well regarded beyond the political elite, able to shape the sentiments of the populace, what Neustadt called that mass "of imprecise impressions held by relatively inattentive people."[9] Power, then, is personal influence; it can only be gained and lost through personal action, and it is interlaced with the president's personality: "What can *this* man accomplish . . . looking toward tomorrow from today."[10]

Neustadt made meaning of the presidency as the focal point for the fluid relationships among the political elite. The skill of the occupant is the key to their success. Influence is personal, and the person in office must help themselves. The game is won and lost by the virtuosic performance of the president as first among equals. If the game can be won by high-minded intellectual argument, all the better. If it must be won by smoke and mirrors, so be it.

Neustadt and Political Science

Neustadt's attempt to make meaning of the presidency happened within a disciplinary moment described in the previous chapter as the rise of behavioralism. Attempts to validate the ideal view of American democracy were being set aside in favor of a dynamic image of political behavior. Political scientists had resolved to study politics via scientific observation rather than philosophical reflection.

Neustadt, a lifelong Democrat, was one of a generation of social scientists drafted into government service during the Second World War. After the war, most in his profession were keen to return to the academy as soon as possible, having grown frustrated with the bureaucratic mind-set of government. Not Neustadt. He relished the practice of politics and the thrill of dealing with real-world problems. But when Republican Dwight D. Eisenhower won the presidency in the 1952 election, Neustadt felt he had to leave Washington, DC. Had Democrat Adlai Stevenson won, he would never have sought to become a professor.[11]

At that time, Neustadt later recalled, there were few opportunities for former White House employees in journalism, law, or business. Neustadt saw academia as one of his few options. Surely he could parlay his first-hand experience with the presidency into a job teaching and writing about it. Like all professional political scientists, Neustadt was not only trying to make meaning; he was also trying to make a living. His book manuscript was his job application. In the professionalized study of politics, his thoughts had to be credentialed by his scientific peers.

This was a challenge. Neustadt found that the professionalized discipline was more focused on validating itself as a science than listening to stories about the Truman White House. His draft manuscript was regarded with suspicion, his experience regarded as irrelevant. "I was almost grudgingly allowed to start at the bottom rung to see if I could satisfy my colleagues that I was serious. But the expectation was that he isn't serious. It was not a benefit to have had the practical experience."[12] Neustadt eventually found a post at Columbia University and set to work on publishing his insights on power in the executive branch.

The presidency literature had been dominated by Edward Corwin's *The President: Office and Powers*, which Neustadt found lacking. Corwin was a scholar of the Constitution—he studied and described the formal powers of the office, how it worked on paper. This was a dying mode of political analysis, and Neustadt was keen to hasten its end. It offered too static a framework to make sense of the dynamic interactions he had seen.

The newer trend was more to his liking: behavioralism. The conceit of this interpretation was that formal structures were mere stage setting for the actions of political players. Their behavior in practice, not theory, must be recorded and understood. In short order, behavioralists would move to the collection of large data sets and begin to deploy theoretical abstractions and hypothesis testing in the mode of the natural sciences. Neustadt would find these later developments baffling. But at this moment, he wondered if he could pitch his stories about the White House as data about how politics really works. Could he convince a publisher that his book was on the cutting edge?

Four presses rejected *Presidential Power* before Neustadt's friend Professor David W. Truman, a leading behavioralist, pulled some strings and had it accepted by John Wiley and Sons.[13] Some academics viewed the manuscript as unremarkable. It says nothing new, said one reviewer for Wiley, and everything it does say is repeated three times. Yet practitioners embraced it and at the highest levels. The new president, John F. Kennedy, was photographed reading it, and its reputation soared. It was assigned in every graduate class on the presidency and taught to generations of undergraduates.

Presidential Power found its way into the thoughts and actions of later presidents. Jimmy Carter told Neustadt he enjoyed the book and wished that in office he had adhered more closely to its teachings. George Ball, an adviser to Kennedy and later Lyndon Johnson, told Neustadt in jest that the book had made his job more difficult. Neustadt had written that presidents should be hypersensitive about their choices. "We used to tell the president what should be done. Now we have to give him *options!*"[14] Jeb Magruder, who would later go to jail for his role in the Watergate break-in and cover-up, told Neustadt that Nixon's chief of staff, Bob Haldeman, had the entire White House staff read *Presidential Power*.[15] Neustadt was unsure what to make of that endorsement.

Neustadt brought a storytelling sensibility to his portrayal of the presidency in action. He set each scene carefully, with meticulous attention to word choice and sentence structure. Writing must be precise and engaging, he believed. He shunned the unstylish approach to prose that characterizes much of modern social science. "So many of us cease to discipline ourselves to write in accessible language," he lamented. "A harder task, to my mind, than writing in professional code, to say nothing of mathematics."[16]

He told stories that invited interpretation, "designed to shed light on a problem."[17] The lessons of each episode he wrote about have assumed, over the years, almost mythic quality. They are folktales of power. "Everyone else looks at politics from far, far away," he said. "I want to snuggle up."[18] Vivid characters populated his book, with the presidents—the peerless operator FDR, tenacious hero Harry S. Truman, passive dolt Dwight D. Eisenhower, macho young prince JFK—at the center of the action.

Neustadt wanted us to see choices as the president saw them: "One must try to view the presidency from over the president's shoulder, looking out and down. . . . We need a frame of reference . . . from the inside out."[19] "He wrote with such clarity that even a journalist could understand it," said David Broder, preeminent political reporter for the *Washington Post*. Broder meant this as a compliment but worried that Neustadt's political science colleagues would use it as a charge of unscholarly conduct.[20]

Vivid writing, strong characters, an inside-out view of a rarely seen world. These are dramatic sensibilities. Little surprise, then, that Neustadt's image of the presidency bursts out of the seams of the most famous modern political fiction.

The West Wing—Presidential power and political fiction

The easy read of Aaron Sorkin's *The West Wing* is that it is a liberal fantasy.[21] Audiences were primed by the time and circumstance of its production to see it that way. *The West Wing* began as Bill Clinton's presidency ended. This intelligent, progressive politician had been soiled by scandal. What could he have achieved with more self-discipline? The show grew ever more popular in the George W. Bush years. The educated classes were alarmed by Bush's anti-intellectualism. They yearned for a scholarly chief executive like Jed Bartlet.

Reread at a distance from the Clinton-Bush years, this "liberal fantasy" decoding seems less compelling. It is instead the relationship between Neustadt and Sorkin that presses itself upon us. Reading *The West Wing* through *Presidential Power* produces a text that is a complex amalgam of majesty and disappointment, of illusory power and persistent weakness. A series of dualisms limn its territory and neatly mirror the tensions in Neustadt's work: responsibility without power, persuasion in place of command, the flawed human in the regal office.

At the core is the figurative king and his court, a deep-rooted cultural schema that the audience is invited to draw upon in interpreting the fiction. In Sorkin's scene-setting pilot episode, the West Wing of the White House is introduced as a palatial series of winding corridors and lushly appointed rooms through which the camera races to keep track of Leo McGarry, the president's chief of staff (the king's adjutant). It is a place of work and of ceremony. A palace and an office building. "I thought I would tell a contemporary story of kings and palaces," says Sorkin. Yet this was not a story of a passive monarch: "I like workplace shows." The West Wing is merely a "very glamourous workplace."[22]

Bartlet, the king, is kept offscreen until the final scene of the episode. He is away on presidential business. The focus is his court, the staffers of the West Wing. The president is referred to only in elliptical terms. The viewer is misdirected into believing he is physically uncoordinated and perhaps intellectually unimpressive.

The premise of the episode is that Josh Lyman, the deputy chief of staff, has made some intemperate comments on a TV talk show. The staff are concerned that the president will discipline him when he returns. It is the wait-till-your-father-gets-home anxiety of children who have misbehaved, the first hint of Sorkin's attraction to strong father figures in his fictions.

When the president finally enters, he is revealed to be a searing intellect and commanding presence. Instead of punishing Lyman, his wayward child, the president dishes out weapons-grade rhetoric in his defense. He demands that Lyman's tormentors, who have come to complain about the staffer, "get out of my house."[23]

The title sequence neatly captures the dual aesthetic of majesty and practicality: each character is shown for a few seconds at work—writing a speech, briefing the press from behind a podium—and then the color image fades to black-and-white, signifying a portrait in a historical archive. These figures are thus placed in our mind as historical actors. We are cued to think simultaneously of their lives lived forward, as they experience the working day, and of their decisions in retrospect, as they will be written of by chroniclers of the Bartlet presidency.

The staff are able yet relatable, at least to an audience used to the discourse of the highly educated elite. Their prosaic workplace conversations shift seamlessly into wonkish policy debates. They wear expensive suits, yet the jackets are off and the ties pulled loose. Sorkin's scripts demand that his characters juggle the elements of his palace/workplace in long conversations composed of rapid exchanges of words, simultaneously luxuriant and staccato. They are choreographed dancers beginning in one part of the palace and then being handed off to a second and sometimes third partner. The viewer is wheeled, on Steadicam, two feet in front of the action. The long single-shot scenes draw together the fragmented concerns of this overworked palace.[24]

The president is Richard Neustadt's ideal: the polymath who must make something of the scattered powers of the presidency. Bartlet is intellectual and decisive. Learned in the literary arts and one of the world's leading economists. Commanding and loyal. Public-facing yet nurturing in private.[25] He is Neustadt's teacher and persuader. "The podium is a holy place for him," Chief of Staff McGarry says. "He sees it as a genuine opportunity to change minds. Also as his way of contributing to the team. He likes teams. I love him so much."[26]

Sorkin wants us to believe that the Bartlet presidency is real, and he gives us a coherent documentation of it week by week. *The West Wing* proceeds chronologically, from one year into Bartlet's first term until the election of his successor and, coherently, with reference in later episodes to earlier events. This placed *The West Wing* at the leading edge of a revolution in television storytelling. Anthology shows, where the events of one episode bear no relation to the events of the next, are designed to be watched in any order so that networks can repeat them at will. Counterfactual histories like *The West Wing* lose their coherence if viewed out of order. The payoff is increased depth of story and character. Episodes of *The West Wing* were like chapters in a novel. Each one drew upon the history established in the last.

As with Neustadt, who told stories about power with the theme of weakness, Sorkin's is the tale of a king pressed upon by foes and events. The struggle of *The West Wing*'s family is to leverage their exceptional gifts in the pursuit of temporary and incremental victories. They see their task as the preservation of the nation and the presidency against the forces of reaction and disorder. It is the effort of a tiny group of the cultural elite to elevate the standards of discourse and to keep the barbarians from the gate.

President Bartlet is politically weak. His approval ratings are referred to on several occasions—42, 48, and a high of 51 percent. This would make Bartlet one of the least popular first-term presidents in modern US history. He was elected without a majority in the popular vote and records "one victory"—placing a justice on the Supreme Court—in his first year in office.[27] This during what should be the most fertile part of his presidency.[28]

Lectured by a retiring liberal Supreme Court justice about his political timidity, Bartlet speaks of the constraints of the presidency:

> I imagine the view from your largely unscrutinized place in history must be very different from mine, but I'd remind you, sir, that I have the following things to negotiate: an opposition Congress, special interests with power beyond belief, and a bitchy media.[29]

Persuasion is the recurrent theme, in its multifaceted Neustadtian form. Deputy Chief of Staff Josh Lyman is tasked with persuasion in private, applying pressure on recalcitrant legislators. Lyman is written as a rough-hewn political operator yet portrayed with softer tones by actor Bradley Whitford. The public face of persuasion comes through Bartlet's pyrotechnical speech making, where his intellect and his passion combine. The speeches are crafted by the soulful draftsman Toby Ziegler and his prodigal assistant, Sam Seaborn.

Bartlet and his staff cycle time and again through compromise, pessimism, and self-restraint, punctuated by vows to be bold. "I live in the world of professional politics," Bartlet says, explaining why he cannot speak his mind on difficult issues. "I'm a human starting gun."[30] He harbors political capital through preemptive accommodation with Republicans. This is the potential danger of Neustadt's concern with future influence: investment is made in a fund that never matures. Toby Ziegler likens the posture of the White House to "walking around as if we know we've already lost."[31]

The frustration comes to a head toward the end of season 1. The president and his chief of staff, old friends and political intimates, are confused about which one of them is restraining the other. "The rumor is I pull you to the center," Leo McGarry says, but "everything you do says: 'For God's sakes, Leo, I don't want to be a one-term president.'" The two work themselves into a lather vowing to speak freely and act more expansively. Martial music plays as the rest of the senior staff accept their new orders with an incantation: "I serve at the pleasure of the president." It is an effective moment, but within a few episodes the old fears and frustrations return. Not only do they "live their lives under siege,"[32] but they also self-indict as exhibiting "a criminally negligent and cowardly refusal to do what we were sent here to do."[33]

Part of the reason Bartlet and his staff are so defensive, feeling so under siege, is that they represent a small elite. The number of significant actors in their political universe is tiny and homogenous: Washington, DC, insiders, who are hyper-verbal and intelligent, politically progressive and drawn from an affluent, coastal, professional class. The rest of the country is portrayed as a backward land. "We lost Texas when you learned to speak Latin," Press Secretary C. J. Cregg says to the president.[34] "Do you know how much noise *Air Force One* makes when it lands in a place like Eau Claire, Wisconsin" is Josh Lyman's threat to an uncooperative congressman.[35] Staffers miss the presidential motorcade during Bartlet's reelection campaign, and a day in Iowa is treated like an expedition to another planet. As a forfeit for a lost bet, Toby Ziegler has to tell everyone he meets that he works in the White House in the expectation that he will be ridiculed or assaulted for saying so.[36]

The West Wing was comparatively successful for a TV show about politics but never became a mass-market juggernaut. Ideology did not hold it back: it forwarded a mostly liberal point of view but nonetheless maintained a bipartisan viewership. It was Sorkin's encoding of the show with the signs of the cultural and educational elite that limited its appeal. *The West Wing* is aimed squarely at a professional class with advanced educations and high incomes.[37] It had a disproportionate influence on ambitious and educated young people, many of whom would become Washington, DC, politicos.

Power without persuasion

There was a romanticism about Richard Neustadt's view of the presidency. Neustadt's lament was how few political scientists followed his lead. As the discipline moved in an ever more technical direction, his influence was confined to a band of adherents engaged in "presidency studies." Neustadt's loose and lucid framework facilitated studies by his followers of presidential personality and decision making, filled with vivid anecdotes and in-depth archival work. They were largely ignored by the rest of US political science, which made meaning of politics through increasingly sophisticated quantitative and deductive methods.

Around the turn of the millennium, the phony war between the approaches ceased. The scientific-rational paradigm, by now dominant in the rest of the American politics subfield, turned its attention to the Neustadtian redoubt of presidency studies. Harvard University methodologist Gary King charged that the Neustadt approach was hopelessly flawed: simply put, there were too few presidents for productive quantitative analysis.[38] The testing of propositions about the presidency ran afoul of the one-president-at-a-time problem. Most social science research effects are comparatively weak: a 10 percent effect of an independent variable on a dependent variable was considered a major result; finding a 20 percent effect might revolutionize the state of knowledge on a particular question. Yet to provide a sufficient data set to show an effect of this size, political scientists would need as many as 638 presidents to study. (At the time of writing, there have been 45.) At this rate, statistically compelling studies of American presidents could begin to be conducted in the year 4378.[39]

Even achieving that dire scenario depended, King continued, on the assumption that there was any solid basis for measuring the factors of character and style that Neustadt placed at the center of his analysis. King was dubious: he saw Neustadtian analysis as based on a lot of anecdote and not much measurement, making it hard to add one study to another in building a repository of knowledge. Having more presidents wouldn't solve the problem if studies of them did not add up to more than a collection of stories.

Stanford University political scientist Terry Moe agreed with Gary King. Moe sought to make meaning of the presidency through the rational choice approach. In Moe's new interpretation, politicians made strict calculations of self-interest, exhibiting none of the variation in style that Neustadt had foregrounded. They behaved in an egoistic way to maximize their power and policy achievement. The tools they needed for success were those of calculation, not persuasion. Moe thought that presidents varied in neither skill nor personality. "Stop thinking about presidents as people," he implored political scientists. Think of them "generically, as faceless, nameless institutional actors."[40]

Moe summed up the Neustadt-dominated studies of the presidency as having "lowly status," "mired in isolation and traditionalism," "inward looking, lacking in rigor." He aimed to impose the scientific-rational view of what constituted good research. By these lights, presidency studies was "falling behind" while the newer approaches "raced ahead." He saw a continued commitment to Neustadt's ideas as close to a pathology: "debilitating . . . obviously deeply rooted." The rational choice "revolution" was coming; it would become "dominant" and "cutting edge."[41] The metaphor was of a forcible takeover: protest or do not, adherents to rational choice assumptions are "coming anyway. They are going to invade presidential studies . . . thrusting. . . . The field is especially fertile ground."[42]

The proclamation by a high-profile figure of a change in how a topic is to be studied creates considerable publication opportunities for other political scientists. Work adopting the new approach can be marketed as novel, part of a revolutionary movement. It fits into a scientific narrative of advancement and, in the discipline's ecosystem, can quickly attract adherents. All aspects of Neustadt's approach now came under attack.

Charles Cameron charged that Neustadt's emphasis on presidential action underplayed the formidable power of the veto. Persuasion was necessary for enacting the agenda of the president, but formal powers, downplayed by Neustadt, were vital to stopping the action of others—in particular, a Congress controlled by the other party. Formal powers like the veto worked entirely separate from the skill and the idiosyncrasies of any specific person in office. Presidents decided when to veto based on a calculation of the distribution of views in Congress, Cameron argued. The threat of the veto was as important as its use. With the veto in play, the legislator at the midpoint of the distribution of views on an issue no longer held sway over the shape of legislation. Instead the representative or senator at the two-thirds point was the key, as two-thirds of members were necessary to overturn a veto. Persuasion did not enter the equation. It was the mathematical calculation of a policy space and the distribution of views within it that determined whether the president would get their way on a piece of legislation.

The next attack on Neustadt came from Kenneth R. Mayer, who took up Gary King's challenge to find more data on presidents. Starting with FDR's time in office, Mayer went through the *Federal Register* and counted the actions presidents took "with the stroke of a pen"—executive orders, proclamations, national security directives, and executive agreements. Stroke-of-a-pen actions were unilateral exertions of presidential power. Persuasion was irrelevant.

Mayer found that, on average, ten to fifteen significant actions were taken by executive fiat each year.[43] These were on major issues of defense and national security (NSC-68, which set the United States' grand strategy for the entire cold war, was a stroke-of-the-pen presidential directive), and on issues where the Congress could not or would not act. (Much of the civil rights progress until the 1964 Civil Rights Act was taken by executive action, in the face of a divided legislative branch.) Mayer concluded that while presidents might prefer major legislation to executive action, the latter was a viable and often-used alternative.[44]

These lines of research combined in the research program of William G. Howell, a student of Moe's. "Presidential research has failed to meet basic standards of research," Howell wrote. He set about rectifying this with his highly influential theory of the unilateral presidency, one in which the president exercises raw power and worries little about persuasion.[45]

The problem with Neustadtian persuasion, in Howell's view, is that it is an intangible activity, a social process that leaves few traces that can be counted, an idiosyncratic activity that looks different every time it happens. It was the stuff of stories, not science. Instead, the president should be viewed as a rational actor, Howell wrote, whose moves leave visible, countable markers in the shape of executive actions. These presidential command prerogatives were the major source of executive strength and not, as Neustadt had contended, acts of weakness.

The president, Howell argued, has what game theorists term *first-mover advantage*: by acting first, the executive creates a new status quo that others must expend time, energy, and political capital to overturn. The president also has the *unified actor* advantage. The president can decide quickly and authoritatively, in sharp contrast to the hundreds of deciders in the legislative branch. Appraising the political moment with clear-eyed calculation, the president can make progress on his agenda by acting at times and on issues of his choosing and outmaneuvering a reactive and divided legislature.

There was not much of this in *The West Wing*, where President Bartlet followed the Neustadt paradigm, rarely using the formal powers of his office. At one point he threatens to nationalize the trucking industry, drafting drivers into military service, but this is a last-resort bluff to try to resolve a labor dispute.[46] It is not until the third season of the show, and Bartlet's third year in office, that the president deploys his veto power. He does so only as a last-ditch gamble after all other measures have failed. "If the House overrides the veto, we are going to look weak," says Josh Lyman. "If the House overrides the veto, we *are* weak," the president responds.[47]

Howell's approach is at the apex of the scientific-rational challenge to presidency studies: there is none of what this new school saw as Neustadt's squishy talk of skill and persuasion, no place for the historian's portrait of the man in office; the flourish of the historical scene is squeezed out by the rigorous tourniquet of algebraic specification.

This is a model of scholarship—and a representation of the presidency—that is unsentimental. The president is "faceless, nameless," a relentless calculating force acting through brute power. The scholarship is concerned with rigor and precision. It is clean and spare, stripped of context and detail. In the rational choice interpretation, it is not important for the president to be a broadly educated humanist, a persuader and compromiser to teach and empathize and cajole. Successful presidents will be clear-eyed calculators of how to maximize their political utilities, to keep the rest of the system on the back foot, to get what they can and push the limits. To deceive and to dominate. To be relentless. To be not Jed Bartlet, but Francis Underwood.

3 | Ambition—*House of Cards*

Looking daggers at the clock on the wall, Congressman Francis J. Underwood knows that time is against him.[1] After twenty-five years in the House of Representatives, he now has a job—majority whip—that suits his talent for bending others to his will. But it is not enough. His ambition burns. He has plans in motion.

He has encouraged a junior congressman, an alcoholic who sees him as a surrogate father, to run for governor of Pennsylvania. The office is vacant; the previous governor left the post to become vice president. On the eve of the gubernatorial election, Underwood finds the congressman passed out from drink, asleep in his car, parked in his garage. Underwood starts the engine, opens the driver's side window, and calmly walks away. "Time would have killed him if I hadn't. Just as it will kill me someday, kill us all."

The next step: Underwood persuades the sitting vice president to return to the Pennsylvania governor's mansion in tribute to the tragic death of the young congressman. There is a vacancy now in the vice presidency. Underwood presents himself to the president as a trusted, seasoned politician available to fill it. He has worked in the dead of night to get here, but, as he reasons, "Ninety-nine percent of this job is in the dark." One step short of the pinnacle of power. One short step, for a calculating, amoral operator like Frank Underwood.

Staring at the clock on the wall, Underwood considers his twisted road to the vice presidency. He has on his desk a weighty hardcover book. It is *The Passage of Power*, from historian Robert Caro's "Years of Lyndon Johnson" series. Caro has devoted his life to the study of LBJ, whom he portrays as a political genius and an animalistic predator. Power is his prey. Caro's books are epic poems about the human urge to bend others to our will. It is no surprise that Frank Underwood picked up a copy.

Passage of Power wasn't placed on Underwood's desk by accident. The creator of *House of Cards*, Beau Willimon, sees the show not just as the story of Underwood, or even as a literal representation of politics, but rather as a rendition of the discourses of power, what it looks like to see unfettered mastery of its brutal ways and means. "The show's not really about politics," says Willimon, a former aide to Democratic luminaries like Howard Dean, Chuck Schumer, and Hillary Clinton. "I'm interested in the dynamics [of power] more than I am in the specifics of a policy issue."[2]

Where *The West Wing* offers a humanist reading of the office, *House of Cards* interprets the presidency as about the cynical calculation of advantage. Where *The West Wing* is about executive weakness, *House of Cards* is about the clear-eyed, coldhearted pursuit of power. Francis Underwood, the protagonist, is a ruthless cynic, possessing few qualities Richard Neustadt would regard as admirable. His focus is tangible action and brute political force. If he deploys persuasion, it is the persuasion of the mailed fist, not the silky speech.

Underwood deploys the full powers of the office in service of his agenda. He seizes disaster relief funds and uses them for his big government jobs program instead. He subverts the National Security Agency to dig up dirt on his political opponents. "I can see you," he tells the television audience. "And I can use what I see to rig the election."[3] He manipulates fears of terrorism and tampers with votes, plunging the electoral process into chaos. "We didn't kill anybody" to get the presidency. "But we would have if it were necessary," he says. The first part of that statement is a lie.

He talks of retaining office for decades: "One nation. Underwood." His ideology, he tells us, is "ruthless pragmatism." It is the only tenable approach afforded by our political system. Polite society needs "someone who will do the unpleasant thing, the necessary thing."[4] Former president Barack Obama, a fan of the show, noted ruefully that President Underwood was "getting a lot of stuff done."[5] Obama was periodically encouraged by his frustrated supporters to be more like Lyndon Johnson, more like Francis Underwood.

In the previous chapter, we saw that Richard Neustadt's view of the persuasive presidency was challenged in political science by an alternate interpretation: the unilateral presidency as the wielder of formidable formal powers. Its underlying logic is that politicians are pure seekers of blunt-force advantage. The origins of that interpretation of American politics—that politicians ruthlessly pursue their self-interest—can be traced to political scientist Joseph A. Schlesinger's study of political careers. Schlesinger wrote in 1965 of politics as *ambition*. The motivating force of all political careers, he posited, is the drive toward higher office.

Schlesinger's ambition theory is paired here with *House of Cards*, the early seasons of which focus on Underwood's rise from Congress to the presidency. Schlesinger's *Ambition and Politics* was published in 1966, when Lyndon Johnson was in the White House, and Johnson connects to *House of Cards* too; he is a clear influence coded into the Underwood character by the producers of the show.

This bundle of intertextual relations—Schlesinger's ambition theory, *House of Cards*, and the career of Lyndon Johnson—is teased out in this chapter in order to produce an interpretation of politics as about ambition. Political science naturalized elite ambition by reducing it to utility-maximizing behavior. Politicians were conceived of as responding rationally to the opportunities created by the political system. You cannot condemn or praise them, proponents of rational choice theory argue, for always looking to the next election, to the chance to move up the political ladder. It is natural for them to do so. Ambition theory became part of the disciplinary construction of the political world. The public should expect neither sincerity nor virtue from its elites but must instead hope that the self-interested maneuverings of the nation's leaders work out so that they serve, by accident, the interests of the people.

Yet introducing the real story of Lyndon Johnson's ambition, as interpreted by Robert Caro, challenges the simple verities of ambition theory. The basic truth of Johnson's life was ambition, as Schlesinger's interpretation would expect. But the details of Johnson's ambition, its volcanic eruptions and sometimes perverse consequences, tell a nuanced story of a man of titanic contradictions. Reading ambition theory through Johnson, and through *House of Cards*, gives us pause about this attempt to interpret the motivations of all politicians through a single assumption.

Ambition and Politics

The political scientist Joseph A. Schlesinger was frustrated by existing studies of politicians, such as Richard Neustadt's, that focused on their individual beliefs and styles. He found himself unable to draw clear direct lines from these idiosyncrasies of personality to actions in political office. He thought that Neustadt's stories of power were interesting anecdotes that didn't amount to much in the way of scientifically validated knowledge. Instead, Schlesinger was convinced that examining the career paths of politicians would reveal their motives and predict their actions.

His work combined the behavioralist focus on tallying the actions of politicians with the rationalist assumption that these actions are driven by utility maximization. Schlesinger collected data on the career paths of significant political figures over a more than forty-year period, recording whether and how successfully each sought to retain their present office or move to a more powerful position.[6] In *Ambition and Politics*, his major work, Schlesinger posited that "man's rise to political power" is the very definition of government. His theory was that it is the seeking of office, not ideology, principles, or deep psychological drives, that is the motive force of political life.[7]

According to Schlesinger, the careers of politicians he studied followed one of three distinct patterns. First was the politician with discrete ambition. They were motivated by holding a particular office for a limited period of time, after which they returned to private life. Second was the politician with static ambition—their goal was to retain their current office for as long as possible. They devoted all their energies to serving existing constituents—those who would determine whether the ambition to hold on to the current office would be achieved. Third was the politician with progressive ambition, who wanted to obtain ever higher office.[8] These politicians would serve current constituents only if doing so helped them toward their next job. They were more concerned with impressing the constituency of the higher office.

Schlesinger posited that variation in ambition type was not caused by ideology or psychology.[9] Schlesinger assumed instead that all politicians were the same, so he focused on the structure of opportunities afforded them by different parts of the US political system. Some offices, Schlesinger believed, afforded the realistic chance for advancement and thus fostered progressive ambition. Precedent was important here; if, in the past, several governors of New York had gone on to be president but no governor of Montana ever had, then the governor in Albany would think seriously about a presidential run and start governing with an eye to their national political profile. They would exhibit progressive ambition. Out in Helena, on the other hand, the Montana governor would have either discrete or static ambition and focus more on home state matters.

Ambition theory fit neatly into the scientific-rational turn in political science.[10] It focused on what politicians did rather than what idealists said they should do. And by positing a universal motivation, one that could be ascribed without much investigation by the researcher, ambition theory held out the promise of rapid research outputs. These could be based on deductive reasoning about motivations and the collection of quantitative evidence. This combination would signify scientific seriousness to the rest of the discipline.

Schlesinger's theory also offered a reassuring naturalization of ambition as something that could be harnessed for the public good. As David Mayhew argued in *Congress: The Electoral Connection*—a defining work focused on the static ambitions of members of the legislative branch—"the reelection quest establishes an accountability relationship with an electorate, and any serious thinking about democratic theory has to give a central place to the question of accountability."[11]

Even progressive ambition, which seems at first glance to challenge the accountability relationship (the politician is eyeing another constituency rather than serving the one that elected them), can be interpreted as morally wholesome. Schlesinger argued that progressive ambition harnesses private goals to public goods by forcing the aspirant to higher office to stand out and to innovate: "If ambition is the motive force in politics, then the leader with progressive ambitions is the hero, the man who brings others together and provides unity and cohesion. If anyone is going to search for solutions, it is the man whose career depends on finding solutions."[12]

Ambition theory remains the default interpretive construct for mainstream political scientists researching the goals of politicians. It is simple, intuitive, and reassuring. Politicians want better jobs, the argument goes, and act so as to get them.

Interpreting *House of Cards*

What cultural resources are relevant to interpreting *House of Cards* and Schlesinger's ambition theory? Let's start with three: Shakespeare, the devil myth, and the life of Lyndon Johnson.

First, the Shakespearean referents. There are several.[13] Kevin Spacey, who played Underwood, adopts the stage techniques of overplayed emotion and gesture rather than the more subtle style of filmed drama. Robin Wright, as his wife, Claire Underwood, is coded as a Lady Macbeth type, complicit in her husband's deeds.

The defining theme of burning ambition is most vividly explored in Shakespeare's *Richard III*. As war gives way to peace at the beginning of *Richard III*, so the pseudo-war of election campaigns gives way to the business of government at the start of *House of Cards*.[14] Plans for the future are set in motion. Relief reigns. "But I . . . ," says Gloucester. I am not relieved, nor satisfied. I did not win the war, am not king. Peace shall not be enjoyed. "I'll make my heaven to dream upon the crown." More than dream. Plot and scheme and strive and scratch. "But I"—the suborning of public life to the private will to power—is our darkest truth about political life.

Shattering the fourth wall, that between actor and audience, is a Shakespearean device. Turning to the camera, both Gloucester and Underwood talk directly to the audience, and none of the other players hears what they say. We are drawn into their conspiracy, with a sly commentary or, sometimes, just a raised eyebrow. Spacey's Underwood is playful. He waves at us from his position at the edge of the frame during the presidential inauguration. When he is bored or exasperated by someone, he shows us with a scowl.

The signs of the devil are printed, too, on Underwood. He is painted in blood tones. We see him first at a diner. Outside, a dog is hit by a car. He walks over, snaps the wounded dog's neck, and returns to his seat for the last lick of flesh from his rack of ribs.[15] Of one of his antagonists, the recalcitrant president of Russia, he says, "I'd push him down the stairs and light his broken body on fire just to watch it burn if it wouldn't start a world war."[16]

He has hellish nightmares. In one, he fights with his wife, pushing her into a full-length mirror. It shatters, and she takes one of the shards and drives it deep into his heart. In another, a young female reporter, a woman he killed on his way to the presidency, gouges out his eyes. She dissolves before him, replaced by the congressman whom Underwood left to die of asphyxiation. "It's just us now," the congressman says. "Rest your eyes. We have all the time in the world."[17] At church, with no one looking, he spits in the face of a statue of Jesus. The statue falls to the ground and shatters. Later he pisses on his father's grave.

Interpreting Underwood by way of Shakespeare and the devil gives us two important access points to his character. But the producers of *House of Cards* make explicit and repeated reference to a much more recent and non-mythological political figure, all but insisting that we read Underwood by way of Lyndon Johnson. By placing *The Passage of Power* so prominently in the shot, the producers also tell us which interpretation of Johnson they want us to use in decoding the fiction: Robert A. Caro's biographies.

Like Francis Underwood, Lyndon Baines Johnson was a Southern Democrat from a poor background. LBJ grew up in the Texas hill country, Underwood in rural South Carolina. Poverty stoked in both of them the burning desire for advancement, disdain of the comfortable elegance of those born to money (what would Lyndon Johnson make of Jed Bartlet?), and empathy for the problems of the poor.

For both men the humiliation of poverty transmogrified into the desire to dominate others. This alchemy meant that both grew into vicious characters. Lyndon Johnson, Caro finds, had a lifelong pattern of needing to boss every room he was in, to lead every organization he was a part of, to use any means to acquire more power. In so doing, he would usually make the organization more effective. And if his personal ambition allied with some compassionate cause—the needs of the poor or the rights of minorities—he would do good.[18]

If his drive for power helped some, it crushed others. Johnson's life, for Caro, is the story of "desperate aggressiveness"; of a "fierce, unquenchable drive"; of "viciousness and cruelty"; of a "joy in breaking backs and keeping them broken" that made "issues impediments and scruples superfluous."[19]

The pattern was set early. LBJ's ninth grade teacher, Mrs. Itz, told Caro of the time the young Lyndon Johnson first spoke of his life's ambition: "All of a sudden, Lyndon looked up at the blue sky and said, 'Someday, I'm going to be President of the United States.' We hadn't been talking about politics or the presidency or anything like that."[20]

In the House of Representatives, to which he was elected in 1937, Johnson despaired of the seniority system, which deprived him of real power. He'd have to wait years to get anywhere in the House—"too long" he said, like Underwood brooding about the clock on the wall.[21] He resolved to run for the Senate.

After two failed attempts, Johnson made it in 1948. The Senate was perfect for his gifts. Johnson was a poor public orator, with his crude manners, his face "a portrait of aggressiveness,"[22] a magnolia accent that raised Northern hackles and African American suspicions. Instead, LBJ was the master of the back room, of the one-on-one meeting where his prey was trapped.[23]

The Senate was such a place. LBJ would rise with unprecedented speed to become leader of his party in the chamber, deploying a go-for-the-throat approach that sliced through the courtly manners of the august institution. "All the time," Caro wrote, "he would be talking, arguing, persuading, with emotion, belief, conviction that seemed to well up inside him and pour out of him—even if it poured out with equal conviction on opposite sides of the same issue."[24]

"I'm just like a fox," LBJ would say. "I can see the jugular in any man and go for it."[25] He would deploy what became known, via testimony from traumatized victims, as the Johnson Treatment. It started with Johnson getting up close. He would grab the victim, often a United States senator or other national figure, by the lapels of their suit jacket. From the other side, a long Johnson arm would snake around the back of the victim's neck. The weight of this heavyset, six-foot, four-inch man would bear down. His head, with its jutting chin, its deep-set, jet-black eyes, its hair slicked back creating the effect of a naked skull, would be thrust from above into the victim's soft, startled features. Conviction would pour out. The grip would be tightened. The vote would be secured.[26]

Ideology didn't matter. The only principle was the pursuit of power. "It's not the job of a politician to go around saying principled things" was Johnson's view.[27] What mattered was the performance of conviction, and LBJ could summon up oceans of it whenever necessary. "You've got to believe what you're selling. What convinces is conviction."[28]

As the 1960 presidential election approached, Johnson had positioned himself for the Democratic nomination. He was Senate majority leader, held in awe by many of his colleagues and regarded as perhaps the most effective holder of that post in US history.[29] His major rival, Massachusetts senator John F. Kennedy, seemed unimpressive. Johnson thought that Kennedy, although young, charismatic, and backed by his family's limitless wealth, was no threat. The majority leader barely saw the junior senator in the chamber and thought him to be a lazy playboy. When LBJ did see JFK, the younger man was bent double with back pain and wore a sickly pallor from Addison's disease. "Malarial," Johnson thought.

So LBJ didn't enter the primaries for the Democratic nomination. He publicly disavowed interest in the presidency, hoping that the party would come to him. Although he tried to hide it, LBJ was terrified of the humiliation of rejection. Kennedy proved formidable beyond Johnson's imagination, winning primary after primary while Johnson's backers pleaded with him to get out of Washington and argue his case. The majority leader bled support, and the junior senator lapped it up. By the time Johnson realized the threat, it was too late, and his last-minute frantic efforts in the final primaries brought about the very humiliation he feared.

Johnson's pursuit of the presidency seemed to be over. Kennedy offered him the vice presidency, and Johnson took it only after performing a macabre calculation of how many presidents had died in office (and thus how likely he was to inherit the throne). He said that being vice president was like being "a cut dog." He had no power, and the humiliation of looking like a hanger-on to Kennedy had cost him his standing back home in Texas. Many around JFK were telling the president that he didn't need Johnson on the ticket in 1964. The vice president's thoughts were dark, then, as he traveled in an open-topped sedan a hundred yards back as the president's car made its way slowly through downtown Dallas on November 23, 1963.[30]

Critiquing Ambition Theory

Thus far I have shown that Francis Underwood is something of a screen counterpart to Lyndon Johnson and that the Underwood character can only be fully decoded by an audience that brings some knowledge of Johnson—as well as Shakespeare and the devil—to the *House of Cards* text.

I must push the argument further, showing that the particularities of Underwood and Johnson suggest gaps in the interpretation of politics as solely about rational ambition. Schlesinger's ambition theory says little of the origins of ambition and of its sometimes self-defeating manifestation. With just a single assumption about what constitutes the character of a politician—the desire for higher office—a full understanding of LBJ, and perhaps of politicians as a class, cannot be achieved.

Lyndon Johnson and his screen counterpart, Frank Underwood, behave in ways that are, at the surface level, in line with ambition theory. They seek ever higher office and act purposively to achieve it. Were they, then, merely normal politicians? Had Caro written thousands of pages and spent a lifetime studying Johnson's personality when he could have just written "politicians seek higher office" and spent his time on another subject?

With Francis Underwood, the conversation is slightly more straightforward, as his deviations from standard political behavior are heightened for dramatic effect. He murders two people—Congressman Peter Russo and the inquiring journalist Zoe Barnes—on his way to the top office. He commits treason and causes the resignation of a president. One can read him as a demonic presence, always shot from below and backlit, spitting on a statue of Jesus that then falls to the ground and shatters; even Satan himself rejects the Underwood soul: "There is no solace above or below," Underwood says. "Only us. Small, solitary, striving, battling each other."[31] It is no great indictment of a social science theory that it fails to account for the presence on television of a fictionalized demon.

But what of Lyndon Johnson? Can ambition theory explain the behavior of this strikingly ambitious man? Only in the coarsest of ways. And here we confront the trade-off forced by the scientific-rationalist interpretation favored by some political scientists. The general pattern of political careers is rendered intelligible by ambition theory. We are armed with a powerful understanding of some of the forces driving our elected representatives and given a salutary, if dispiriting, reminder that most of the high-flown rhetoric of the politician can almost always be translated as "I'd like to first keep my current job and then move to a more powerful one."

But the particularities of the Johnson character challenge ambition theory. The linear nature of Schlesinger's theory might blind us to the messiness of individual passions and the capacity of humans to engage in self-defeating (or self- and other- elevating) behavior. Caro's excavation of LBJ's soul shows a man caught in a deep conflict between his towering ambition and his terror of public humiliation.

On several crucial occasions in his career, the combination so distorted LBJ's calculations of risk and reward as to muddy the clean waters of ambition theory. Elected to the House of Representatives in 1937, LBJ launched a long-shot bid to leave right away and was defeated in the Democratic senatorial primary of 1941. Seven years later, LBJ made a long-shot bid again. His decision to run was, in Caro's telling, utterly irrational. He was up against a heavy favorite in Coke Stevenson, and had he lost, he would have had to leave Washington, his political career over.

Few rational politicians, coolly calculating the probabilities, would have taken this risk, but to Johnson, being one of a crowd in the House was worse than anything, worse than leaving politics completely. "He had to try for the Senate," Caro writes. "However great the sacrifice he might have to make—the sacrifice of his House seat—to enter the Senate race, however long the odds against him in that race might be, he had to enter."[32] He almost certainly committed electoral fraud to win, the contemporary discovery of which would have cost him not only his political career but likely his liberty too. The smooth calculations of rational ambition theory seem hard to reconcile with this episode in the life of Lyndon Johnson.

Later, too, Johnson's inner turmoil would interfere with the rational servicing of his ambition. As the fight for the 1960 Democratic presidential nomination heated up, LBJ refused to enter the primaries or to campaign against JFK for the nomination. Caro finds that Johnson was crippled by the fear of being seen to try and failing; his risk aversion in this instance was as powerful as his risk acceptance in entering the 1948 Senate race. At just the point that Kennedy was poised to lock up the nomination, Johnson launched himself on the campaign trail and begged and pleaded for support. As the inevitable loss came, LBJ had brought about the very humiliation he feared.[33]

Frank Underwood's achievement of his ambition is postponed over two delicious seasons of plotting. We are complicit in the conspiracy as Underwood turns to the camera, looks right at us, and reaches through the screen to grab our hands and dip them in the blood he has spilled. At the moment of climax, he stands on the brink of the Oval Office with his wife, Claire. She has bought him a ring to commemorate his ascension to the presidency, the completion of this masterwork on which they have toiled together. She tells him to go in, alone. "Take a few moments for yourself."

Over the threshold, at the desk. The stately chair pushed aside contemptuously. Palms laid flat on the oak surface. Power soaking through his skin. Deep breaths. Suddenly the president of the United States looks straight into the camera and with two quick jabs pounds his ring into the desk, gunshots that echo across the realm he now rules.[34]

"One nation. Underwood."

Ambition and Character

One of the most persistent interpretations of politics is that it is about ambition. Our lushest literature and some classic political science theories share this reading. In Shakespeare, in Caro, and in *House of Cards*, ambition is studied through the excavation of individual hopes and fears, seeking to account for what is unique to the individual and what is general to human nature. Yet other human characteristics become apparent as an individual is dissected. The will to power clashes with the fear of humiliation. The strategic thinker struggles with the urge to self-harm. The calculator of advantage struggles with their animal passions.

In the scientific-rational approach to political science, ambition is presented as a stark calculation of risk and reward, a lean and rigorous way of organizing observations about political behavior. The idiosyncrasies of character are viewed as irrelevant. This assumption produces one-dimensional interpretations of politics. We are led to see the political elite as driven by this single thing that cannot be judged good or bad but is instead a natural law of public life. Ambition theory is a useful fiction, but what is the cost of circulating this image of our leaders? We are left unable to see them as humans, to empathize with and criticize as we would other responsible figures in our lives. And might not our politicians themselves internalize this schema of how they should behave, making self-fulfilling prophecies of our darkest fears about their motivations?

The inquiry into character and its complexities, contrasted with the scientific imperative to make meaning of politics as an activity with simple motivational roots, continues in the next chapter. Can the scientific-rational approach help us make meaning of that most vivid collision of human weakness with public responsibility: the politics of scandal?

4 | Character—*Scandal*

"Anything is fixable." That is the mantra of Olivia Pope, the crisis manage-ment guru portrayed in the political fiction *Scandal*. She often follows up with a firm "It's handled." The philandering, the corrupt, and the murder-ous among the Washington, DC, elite long to hear those reassuring words. *Scandal* is a complementary fiction to *House of Cards*. Both imagine the political class as cynical and ruthless seekers of advantage in an intra-elite game. Killers, metaphorically and, in these hyperbolic fictions, literally.

A common political science approach to scandalous behavior is to ra-tionalize it as political advantage seeking, to gather data on its effects on careers, and to design incentive structures to minimize its occurrence. Private compulsions and irrational motivations are rendered invisible. The rational climber of ambition theory is also the rational wrongdoer of scandal scholarship.

In the previous chapter, an excavation of Lyndon Johnson's ambition suggested some missing pieces in James Schlesinger's political science theory. Here we look closely at Gary Hart, the charismatic front-runner for the 1988 Democratic presidential nomination who was undone by an alleged affair with a young model. Hart's story suggests that by construct-ing an image of politicians as rational actors, political scientists might be underplaying the characterological wellsprings of malfeasance. This ratio-nal interpretation serves scientific aims and allows us to trace the impact of scandals on political fortunes, but it offers a thin understanding of why politicians commit outrageously risky scandalous acts in the first place.

By dismissing inquiries into character as unscientific "soul stuff," the scientific-rational interpretation risks resigning political science from one of the most important questions facing citizens: how should they weigh and judge the human foibles of their leaders, both those in office and those seeking office? With political science having largely recused itself from these questions, the media fills the gap. Yet the media has commercial in-centives. They are driven by ratings imperatives as much as (and even more than) the public interest. Fictions like *Scandal*, political science attempts to naturalize scandalous acts as rational advantage seeking, and the media's treatment of the issue does not provide citizens with a means of judging what traits and acts are truly injurious to the discharge of public office. To dig into this issue, we must first reexamine the case of Gary Hart.

Monkey Business

Indignant and exposed, Gary Hart stands before a room packed with TV anchors and print news reporters.[1] It is May 6, 1987, primary season in the race to succeed Ronald Reagan as president of the United States. The Colorado senator is the front-runner for the Democratic nomination. In the Hanover Inn, on the campus of New Hampshire's Dartmouth College, Hart is half blinded by TV lights and flashbulbs. Without a lectern to shield him, the physical distance between the Colorado senator and the assembled press can be measured at about six feet. But the metaphorical distance between the public and private life of this cerebral and introverted man is about to be reduced to zero.

"Senator," begins Paul Taylor of the *Washington Post*, "do you believe adultery is immoral?" In an earlier time, cocky and irreverent and possessed of a memorable turn of phrase, Hart had said that he believed in "reform marriage."[2] He had separated from his wife, Lee, on more than one occasion, although each time they had patched things up. He had often been seen in the company of other women.

"Yes," Hart replied, he believed that adultery was immoral. The scandal roiling Hart's campaign during this week in May concerned Donna Rice, a twenty-nine-year-old model and actress from Miami. During a break from the campaign, Hart had taken her on a pleasure cruise around Bimini, an island fifty miles off the coast of Florida. They kept in touch, and she had flown to Washington, DC, to see him. Journalists from the *Miami Herald* were tipped off about the senator and the model, who were spotted entering and exiting Hart's townhouse.

Now, under intensive questioning from Taylor, Hart began to panic. *What was going on?* He knew Paul Taylor. They had, in Taylor's words, "hit it off." They'd had dinner, talked about policy. Taylor was, by his own lights, a "good cop" journalist. He would compliment the politicians he wrote about, ingratiate himself with them, learn about their ideas.[3] But now, Hart thought, he was asking such personal questions, crossing the line, breaking the unwritten rule.

Paul Taylor saw it differently. In his proudest moments, Taylor saw himself following in the tradition of Joseph Pulitzer, who had written in 1904 of the journalist as "a lookout on the bridge of the ship of state . . . peer[ing] through the fog and storm to give warning of the dangers ahead."[4] Today Taylor had abandoned his watch on the ship of state in favor of peering into a yacht named *Monkey Business*, the vessel that took Hart and Rice cruising around Bimini. The warning he was sounding was that Gary Hart, leading candidate for the highest office in the land, had vacationed with a woman who was very definitely not his wife.

"Have you ever committed adultery?" Taylor pressed. Under the glare of the lights at the New Hampshire press conference, Hart tried to end the inquisition. "Ahh," he ventured, "I do not believe that is a fair question. . . . You can get into some very fine distinctions."

Twenty-four hours earlier Hart had tried to deflect the scandal, to make it about the press themselves. In an address to the American Newspaper Publisher Association, Hart told the assembled journalists to take seriously their "enormous power" and "heavy responsibility" to uphold the standards of elevated discourse. The stakes were "not one person's public career, but a nation's public life." Warming to his theme, Hart invited the reporters to "ask yourselves some searching questions about what is right and what is truthful . . . about whether the urgency of meeting a deadline is subordinate to hearing the truth; and about whether it`s right or good journalism to draw an extraordinary conclusion before hearing some rather ordinary facts."

Seeking to put the matter to rest, Hart had concluded with a rhetorical flourish: "Did I make a mistake by putting myself in circumstances which could be misconstrued? Of course I did," Hart said. "But did I do anything immoral? I absolutely did not."[5]

Taylor had brooded over that speech and decided to take it as a direct challenge. "The nakedness of his deceit put me in an uncharitable frame of mind," he later wrote. Taylor drove over to the press conference flushed and exhilarated.[6] Hart, after all, had raised the broad, nebulous concept of morality. The candidate had already drawn his petard and begun the self-hoisting. Taylor would merely help him complete the operation.

TAYLOR: It seems to me that the question of morality was introduced by you.

HART: That's right. That's right.

TAYLOR: And it's incumbent upon us to know what your definition of morality is.

HART: Well, it includes adultery.

TAYLOR: So you believe adultery is immoral.

HART: Yes, I do.

TAYLOR: Have you ever committed adultery?

The room was suddenly still. "Hart was standing no more than six feet from me," Taylor recalls.[7] "We both had trouble keeping our voices from breaking, and neither of us spoke much above a whisper." Looking into the senator's eyes, Taylor saw a "wild look of hurt, bewilderment, and god-awful betrayal."

Taylor had gone too far to stop now: "Can I ask you whether you and your wife have an understanding about whether or not you can have relationships, you can have sexual encounters with . . ."

Hart: "My inclination is to say no, you can't ask me that question, but the answer is no, we don't have any such understanding. We have an understanding of faithfulness, fidelity, and loyalty."

In the frenzied aftermath of the press conference, Hart realized that his dreams of winning the presidency were over. Within a couple of days, the *Washington Post* had the name of a second woman who, they claimed, was in a long-term relationship with Hart. A third woman with whom Hart had had an assignation told the senator she would kill herself if reporters came to her door. For Hart the whole thing was a "nightmare. . . . We were in some kind of Oz land. For years and years after, people would stop me in airports and say, 'You should have stayed in the race.' I mean, they had no idea. They had *no idea*."[8] Hart turned to his press secretary, Kevin Sweeney: "This thing is never going to end, is it? "Let's go home."[9]

Gary Hart would never escape the shadow of the scandal. "This whole business of '87 is flypaper to me," he told reporter Matt Bai in 2003. "It's so frustrating. It's like being in a time warp. I want to get unstuck."[10] The media, too, would thereafter operate in a changed world. Private lives were now seen as legitimate areas of public concern. The "character issue" became central to political reporting. Journalist Paul Taylor would also feel forever stuck in that moment in the Hanover Inn. "It was the right question to ask, and it was the right topic to raise," he later recalled. "But if it never gets asked again, no one will be happier about that than me."[11]

For Matt Bai, who exhumed the story more than twenty-five years later, this was the moment everything changed, "the week politics went tabloid." Henceforth, Bai argues, politicians were treated more as "flawed celebrities" than statespeople, and, in that New Hampshire inn, "the worlds of public service and tabloid entertainment, which had been gradually orbiting closer to one another, finally collided."[12]

Scandal

The Hart episode signifies the collision between politics and entertainment, of high affairs of state and low matters of salaciousness. We can draw a direct line from this real-world drama to the political fiction *Scandal*.

The message of *Scandal* is that Washington, DC, is full of greedy and immoral people whose public presentation is a façade. Creator Shonda Rhimes saw the nation's capital as a place "where people said these wonderful things but behind closed doors were monsters."[13] Their misdeeds are covered up by others in the elite, such as crisis management consultants like Olivia Pope, who make money by cleaning up the politicians' messes. *Scandal* resonates because it reflects the broken boundaries of the public and the private, politics and entertainment and media, in the post–Gary Hart age.

Scandal is the most watched of our political fictions, being for a time the number one drama on any network and scoring especially highly with the coveted eighteen-to-forty-nine-year-old demographic.[14] It reimagines the genre of televised political fictions. If *Scandal* is one part *West Wing*, it is three parts daytime soap opera. There is very little actual policy discussed in the show. The meaning making comes from the nature of its characters. They are simultaneously self-interested and wildly out of control, at the mercy of narcotic substances like power, greed, and love, driven to outrageous acts. Their internal drives and passions gush out all over the place. The show validates our hunch that the cool mask of the politician melts, behind closed doors, to reveal a ravenous monster.[15]

Joshua Malina, who starred in both *Scandal* and *The West Wing*, explains the difference between the shows. On *The West Wing*, Malina recalls, presidential assistant Sam Seaborn begins dating an escort and seeks to rescue her from her poor life choice—a classic Sorkinian male hero fantasy. If this story line ran in *Scandal*, Malina said, Seaborn would have had the escort killed to keep the relationship quiet.

Shonda Rhimes crafted a hyperkinetic show, full of quick cuts (accompanied by a staccato camera flash effect that calls to mind swarming paparazzi) and gyrating plot twists. There were clever intertextual referents. Contemporary news stories were mashed up and satirized, such as the fictional sexting congressman Redwood Johnson, a story line that ran soon after the real-world Anthony Weiner scandals, wherein the former New York congressman was revealed to have sent intimate pictures to a supporter via Twitter. In another plot, an Edward Snowden type comes to Olivia Pope & Associates with details of unauthorized government surveillance programs, a story he narrates while the gloriously incongruous 1970s R&B hit "Carwash" plays on the soundtrack.

Rhimes was sanguine when the show was called ridiculous: she aimed for grand emotion, not political realism. But she objected when *Scandal* was dismissed as having nothing to say.[16] Indeed *Scandal* shares significant similarities with our corpus of political fictions. Its focus is on the power elite, and its conceit is to show us their actions behind the scenes. Its subject is governance, albeit governance refracted through private psychopathology rather than public policy.

Scandal is a fiction about the public enactment of private drives. It is an interpretation of political malfeasance focused on character. How has our other interpretive construct—political science—made meaning of scandal?

Scandology: The Political Science of *Scandal*

British scholar Anthony King called the scientific study of political malfeasance "scandology." He saw it as the study of the intersection of money, sex, and power. Scandology is the attempt by political scientists to apply the principles of scientific-rationalism—define an activity precisely, cast it as the actions of strategically motivated elites, and collect a lot of data—to an area that seems resistant to systematic study. Scandals are hard to define, they excite passion and panic, and there are relatively few of them. If the scientific-rational approach can make sense of scandals, it has passed a high hurdle.

Scandologists think of three types of actors playing a "scandal game": the transgressor (who commits the scandalous act), the media (who publicizes it), and opposition politicians (who seek political or legal punishment of the transgressor). Scandologists explain media and opposition responses to scandal via an assumption of rationality. Although they usually say less about the motivation for the initial scandalous act, it might similarly be seen as a self-interested response to the opportunities and challenges present in a given political environment.[17]

In this vein, political scientists Scott Basinger and Brandon Rottinghaus conceive of scandals as a series of choices made by the various players based on their calculation of their best move given what the other parties are likely to do. They seek to derive a generic logic of presidential scandals. First assume that a president accused of transgression has a 50 percent chance of having actually committed a transgression—they may be innocent or guilty. Then assume that the media publicizes an allegation.

The president then has two options: "tell all" and turn over the evidence as to their innocence or guilt, or "stonewall"—deny everything. The media then has its own choice: to accept what the president says or to pursue and investigate. Each choice, Basinger and Rottinghaus argue, is based on the president or the media anticipating the move of the other side. Imagined in this way, scandals operate on the same logic as any other strategic interaction: each side wants the best outcome for itself at the least cost.

Brendan Nyhan, too, sought to understand the logic of scandals by thinking of them as games of iterative play. Nyhan was interested in why some presidential transgressions became scandals and others went unnoticed. He found that much of the time the answer was obvious: the transgression was either too minor to be worthy of attention or so spectacular that a scandal was inevitable. The interesting cases, Nyhan argued, were those in the middle ground of scandalousness.[18] What led the political opposition to try to make a scandal out of some of these borderline instances and not others?

Nyhan's answer was that the opposition makes a bet about the vulnerability of the president. A popular first-term president is simply too strong a target. The scandal will either not catch fire or rebound upon the opposition who tried to foment it.[19] An unpopular or second-term president is much more likely to be hit with scandal. As the public either doesn't like or is growing tired of them, the opposition is able to fan the flames of any wrongdoing. Nyhan's data supported this, and his explanation was that the opposition acted rationally: scandals were "politics by other means" and made for an especially attractive weapon when the intended target was weak.[20]

Scientific rationalists are mostly satisfied, then, that large chunks of scandal-related behavior by the political opposition and the media can be understood by assuming everyone is acting to maximize their utility. But they have less to say about the transgressor themselves. Some forms of scandalous behavior—such as enriching oneself or one's friends, or enhancing one's chances of gaining and retaining power—are rational if the transgressor assumes they will not be caught and punished.[21] One could construct a rationality-based story about Richard Nixon's Watergate transgressions, for example, centered on his desire to retain power. But Nixon was going to win the 1972 election in a landslide anyway, and if he wanted to play dirty tricks, there were ways he could have kept the operation away from the White House or simply killed the story soon after it broke with a low-cost admission of wrongdoing. Surely either option would have been more rational than engaging in the rolling cover-up that led to his impeachment and resignation.

Sex scandals such as the Gary Hart affair are even more difficult to understand through the lens of scientific rationality. One could simply keep extending the rationality principle beyond the political sphere and into private drives such as lust, but this creates a contradiction between types of utility maximization: privately rational lust-satisfying behavior is publicly irrational political behavior. And if satisfying lust is the objective, then surely a rational actor would do so in the way least likely to make political trouble. Many scandal-prone politicians seem to choose partners and create situations that maximize, rather than minimize, their political peril. This suggests that meaning cannot be made of scandals through the rationality frame alone.

What about the voting public? How do they respond to scandals? This is a complicated issue. Consider this voter, interviewed about the Gary Hart scandal by the *PBS NewsHour* in 1987:

> WOMAN: Well, I think his private life is his own business.
> INTERVIEWER: It wouldn't affect whether or not you would vote for him?
> WOMAN: Yeah, it makes a big difference to me.
> INTERVIEWER: His private life does?
> WOMAN: Yes.
> INTERVIEWER: Should the press report on his private life?
> WOMAN: No.
> INTERVIEWER: How are you going to know about it?
> WOMAN: I would have felt better if I didn't know about it.
> INTERVIEWER: You don't want to know?
> WOMAN: No, I don't.
> INTERVIEWER: But it does affect the way you vote, right?
> WOMAN: It certainly does.[22]

The impact of scandal on public opinion is, anecdotally at least, quite confusing. The scientific response to this is to look for a way to quantify the problem. Scandologists have concentrated their efforts on two questions: (1) what does the experience of scandal do to a politician's chances of reelection? and (2) how does a scandal shift voters' evaluation of the qualities of a candidate?

The best studies of how scandals shape elections have not been of presidents; there are too few presidential elections tainted by scandal to find significant patterns. Instead, scandologists have turned to the more numerous elections to the House of Representatives. Rodrigo Praino, Daniel

Stockemer, and Vincent Moscardelli combed through the records of the House Ethics Committee in every Congress from 1972 to 2006, tallying investigations of an incumbent accused of scandalous behavior. Then they looked at how these members fared compared to non-tainted representatives. (See table 1.)

Table 1

Outcome	Scandal Races	Non-Scandal Races
Won general election	43 (48.9%)	6,657 (86.5%)
Defeated in general election	12 (13.6%)	304 (4%)
Resigned/retired	23 (26.1%)	653 (8.5%)
Defeated in primary election	90 (11.4%)	79 (1%)
Total	88 (100%)	7,693 (100%)

An incumbent who steers clear of scandal and stands for reelection is successful nineteen times out of twenty. Hit by scandal, their prospects plummet: they are returned to Congress only half of the time. Some are so wounded they do not even attempt to win another term, resigning or retiring instead. Others are defeated by their opponent in the general election or by another candidate from their own party in a primary.

Working with a more expansive definition of wrongdoing, political scientist Scott Basinger identified 250 post-Watergate congressional scandals (almost three times the 88 identified by Praino and his colleagues). His conclusions were similar: becoming embroiled in a scandal is one of the few ways in which an incumbent in the House loses an election. Basinger calculates that 40 percent of those hit by scandal are not returned to the next Congress and that a scandal costs an incumbent an average of 5 percent of the vote at the next election.

All is not lost for the scandal-hit House member, though. They still have a roughly 50 percent chance of winning the next election and, according to the Praino team's data, they recover two-thirds of the lost vote in the second post-scandal election. By the time the third election comes along, it is as if the scandal never happened. Scandologists can thus quote a firm price to members of the House of Representatives engaging in wrongdoing: if you are caught, it will cost you 5 percent of the vote and the stench will linger for six years.

There are far fewer presidential scandals, so statistical overviews are less valuable when talking about the executive branch. The three most significant presidential scandals of the modern era hit second-term presidents, so the question of reelection did not arise. Watergate gained public traction after Nixon had won a second term, as did the Iran-Contra affair for Reagan and the Monica Lewinsky scandal for Clinton.

Lacking data on presidential reelection outcomes, scandologists have used proxy measures such as approval ratings. Much of this analysis has focused on the Clinton/Lewinsky scandal, which happened in the modern era of saturation polling and sprawled into a yearlong saga, giving scandologists a lot of data to work with.

Yet the data are confusing. Hit by confirmed allegations of misconduct while in office, with blanket coverage by the media, the political opposition, and a highly aggressive special prosecutor, Clinton nonetheless maintained solid approval ratings. As the House voted to impeach him and the Senate put him on trial, public approval of his job performance remained in the mid-60 percent range.[23] How did he manage this?

One hypothesis is that the public was simply not as willing to deal in blanket moral judgments as Clinton's opponents hoped. Partisanship certainly mattered; after the scandal broke, 64 percent of Republicans said Clinton should leave office, compared to only 12 percent of Democrats and 33 percent of independents.[24]

But more than reflexive partisan bias was at work. Polling data showed that the public held a nuanced view of what constitutes a good president. Clinton's ratings as a moral leader collapsed from around 50 percent before the Lewinsky scandal to around 30 percent after the news broke.[25] Yet two other key dimensions—perceptions of Clinton as a strong leader and as compassionate—remained unaffected by the scandal. Political scientist Arthur H. Miller found that the public weighted strength and compassion more heavily than morality when considering their approval of the president. Only voters on the far right considered the morality question to be overwhelmingly important.[26]

Gary Hart, one imagines, would be equally amused and chagrined by another finding from the Clinton imbroglio: 60 percent of the public agreed that the best way to avoid a repeat of this kind of scandal was to make sure that a president's private life remains private.[27] Using data collected by the National Election Study, political scientist Laura Stoker investigated why Hart had been destroyed by scandal while Clinton had survived. As with studies of Clinton, Stoker found that voters did pay attention to the Donna Rice scandal and downgraded their assessments of Hart as a moral leader as a result. Partisanship was a huge factor. Democrats, even morally conservative Democrats, judged Hart much less harshly than Republicans.

The most significant predictor of attitudes toward Hart was the political sophistication of the respondent. Those with high levels of previous political involvement, and who were knowledgeable about policy, cared less about Hart's private affairs. Those without much prior involvement in politics weighed the scandal more heavily, and it drove them to a negative evaluation of Hart. This, of course, was a much bigger problem for Hart than for Clinton; the Colorado senator was a presidential candidate, not an incumbent, so he had had much less opportunity to create a positive impression of his job performance when the Rice scandal hit.[28]

The Character Issue

Pairing *Scandal*, the fiction, with scandology, the political science approach to the phenomena, allows us to consider the meaning made by both. The political science critique of the television show *Scandal* is that it is unrealistic. In the scientific-rationalist view, the political elite are more careful and more serious than the show's portrayal of them. Yet fiction is, by design, a heightened and stylized representation of a world. At issue is the usefulness of the fiction in thinking about the political world rather than its literal truth.

Scandal focuses on affairs of the bedroom, and it is these salacious misdeeds that pose the most significant challenge to the scientific-rational representation of politics. An advantage-seeking explanation for money and power scandals can be constructed, especially if the scandalous behavior is competently executed and the politician has a reasonable expectation of getting away with it. But scandals that bring public ruin for sexual or romantic motivations are harder to understand from the scientific-rational angle. Why would a utility-maximizing politician pursue such suboptimal behavior? These matters are difficult to model scientifically and are often left out of the political science construction of the politician.

Addressing this gap implicates the question of character, that bundle of manifest and suppressed drives and urges. Consultant and former political operative Judy Smith, the real-world inspiration for the Olivia Pope character, has one overarching rule for how to manage crises: don't get into them in the first place. Smith sees a common thread among her clients: the problems are self-inflicted. We are all bundles of potent personality traits such as ego, denial, fear, and ambition. These are the wellsprings of success and of ruination. The key, Smith argues in her self-help book *Good Self, Bad Self*, is to exercise self-awareness and self-policing.[29]

Journalists such as Paul Taylor and Tom Fiedler, the tormentors of

Gary Hart, agree. They thought that Gary Hart's character, his values and lack of self-control, was illuminated by the Donna Rice episode. When asked whether Hart's private life was legitimate public business, Fiedler asks, "What should we have done at that moment? Should we have closed our notebooks and caught the next plane back to Miami, concluding that reporting the lie [Hart's denial of any relationship with Rice] wasn't newsworthy?"

Fiedler's argument is that it is for the voters to determine whether they care about a politician's private life. The media's job is to find the facts and publish them. Some voters, Fiedler continues, might not care much at all. But for others—in Fiedler's view "the great majority" of voters—such information is crucial to their choices. "This is the much-discussed character issue," he writes. "It goes to the essence of the candidate; it's about authenticity, empathy, integrity, fairness and more. Issues change, and with them the candidate's positions. But character doesn't change, at least not much. For a journalist to withhold information that more fully reveals the character of a candidate would, in my opinion, be a sin of omission."[30]

For Paul Taylor, by the 1988 campaign, questions of should or should not had already been overtaken by the realities of modern media. Personality and image became central to politics, because, in the age of television and celebrity gossip magazines, they were central to the larger culture in which politics is embedded. Politicians are not blameless in this, Taylor argues. They take advantage of television by making personality more central to their campaigns than policies and issues. Probing the veracity of autobiographical claims becomes, then, a matter of exposing hypocrisy.[31]

Matt Bai, who exhumed the Gary Hart scandal a quarter century later, has a more dyspeptic view. He sees the Gary Hart affair as the culmination of some ugly trends in journalism, not all of which are motivated by the public-spiritedness to which Fiedler lays claim nor excusable by Taylor's we-didn't-start-it defense. The journalists who pursued Hart were part of the post-Watergate generation, Bai notes. They had drawn two conclusions from that time. First, politicians were untrustworthy, and therefore the cozy relationships some journalists had with roguish figures like John F. Kennedy had to stop. Kennedy's promiscuity and drug taking had posed serious threats to national security.[32] Lyndon Johnson had lied about his intentions in the Vietnam War, and Richard Nixon had lied about both Vietnam and Watergate. Post-Watergate journalists were ashamed of their predecessors' complicity in these episodes. They compensated with a feverish devotion to exposing the lies of the political elite.

The second post-Watergate lesson was that the investigative reporters who broke the scandal, Bob Woodward and Carl Bernstein, had become famous. Every young reporter wanted to break the next Watergate, be professionally revered, and maybe even have a movie star play them in a Hollywood blockbuster.[33]

Further, a "new journalism" associated with the likes of Hunter S. Thompson and driven by wild narratives and a colorful sideways look at politics (especially political campaigns) had replaced the staid and factual reportage of mid-century. New journalism was free with speculation and interpretation and neatly dovetailed with the psychoanalytic turn in American psychology (and pop psychology). Sigmund Freud and Erik Erikson, with their theories of the volcanic forces bubbling beneath the surface of the be-suited candidate, were touchstones for these wannabe Woodwards and would-be Bernsteins.[34]

As political science trended toward constructing politicians as one-dimensional strategic actors without a hinterland, political journalism was going in the other direction, delving deeper into psychoanalysis and private lives. Richard Ben Cramer summed up the sensibilities of those reporters trailing the candidates in the 1987–1988 cycle: they had become "character cops." On the campaign trail, the press corps were "rooting up the forest floor, like hogs after a truffle, snouting out" the candidates' characters.[35] The "drum majorette" of the character cops was *Vanity Fair*'s Gail Sheehy. In an extraordinary article published months after Gary Hart dropped out of the race, Sheehy proposed a kind of grand psychoanalytic theory of the candidate.

Hart was, she proclaimed, a compulsive risk taker determined to destroy himself. A "pathological deficit in Hart's character" doomed him, driving him to seek out extramarital liaisons to "appease the inner dictator of his sore guilty soul." Schooled in a rigid and controlling religious environment, with a mother who alternated between taking to her bed with fake illnesses and manically scrubbing the family home to a fastidious shine, Hart's psyche could not develop normally. Sheehy draws her conclusions:

> Here is a man who grew up in a severely restricted manner, by virtue of his religion, his social milieu, and a mother whose treatment of her son was tantamount to child abuse. Emotionally deformed by that long boyhood, simply not equipped with any understanding of or feeling for the value built into human relationships. . . . One side of Hart, the rigid and controlling spirit of his Fundamentalist past, seeks perfection and inflicts harsh self-punishment for any

natural pleasure. . . . The other side of him, the passionate and pro-
fane side, never saw the light of day as an adolescent boy—indeed,
was imprisoned for his first twenty-five years. That delinquent side
began beating on the cell floor and going over the wall. . . . Finally,
it went haywire.[36]

For political scientists of the scientific-rational persuasion, questions of character are fraught. Character is a nebulous concept, hard to
define and hard to measure. What a politician does—their behavior—is
outwardly observable. But the inner reasoning behind that behavior is
invisible.[37]

Political scientists have therefore mostly downplayed the question of
why politicians engage in scandalous behavior—especially sex scandals—
and focused instead on the aftermath: the electoral consequences, the media's coverage of the scandal, the strategy for dealing with a scandal. The
reason for this is simple: the rationality assumption, by definition, cannot
imagine self-defeating behavior.[38]

If, as a rule, political scientists try to avoid the study of character, the
exception is James David Barber. Barber thought that political science
should be of public service, and the greatest public service would be to
answer one question: how can we predict presidential performance in the
White House? His vision of political science was one where the interpretation of politics was driven by the needs of society rather than the disciplinary desire for scientific legitimacy.[39]

Barber looked beyond the surface of political campaigns—the policies
and issues and advertisements—to seek clues about the whole person, to
assess a candidate for high office as "a human being like the rest of us," a
person applying for the job of president.[40]

Like Richard Neustadt, Barber addressed a political science at the start
of its behavioral revolution. Staid analysis of constitutional texts was out
and, like Neustadt, Barber agreed that the behavior of the political elite
should be the focus of attention. The revolution had yet to take the big
data–abstract rationality turn, and so again like Neustadt, Barber found
himself briefly on the cutting edge of the discipline and then quite quickly
forgotten in favor of strict assumptions of elite rationality.

Also like Neustadt, Barber grew frustrated with the reluctance of his
colleagues to consider character as a factor in potential performance in
the Oval Office. "The president is not some shapeless organism," he wrote
in his book *Presidential Character*, "but a man with a memory in a system
with a history. Like all of us, he draws on his past to shape his future. The

pathetic hope that the White House will turn a Caligula into a Marcus Aurelius is as naïve as the cliché that ultimate power inevitably corrupts."[41] Instead, Barber thought, the major determinant of presidential performance would be the presidential character, their inner motivations and personal style as it interacts with the political world.

Barber wanted to develop a general theory of presidents, but he spent most of his scholarly efforts interpreting one kind of political personality, which he saw as compulsive and likely to engage in self-defeating behavior. Woodrow Wilson, for example, had displayed a stubborn refusal to compromise that had cost him his chance to pass the League of Nations treaty through the US Senate. Herbert Hoover fixated on keeping government out of the economy despite the catastrophic market failures of the Great Depression. And Lyndon Johnson persisted in a failing Vietnam policy regardless of mounting evidence of its disastrous consequences.

When first published, Barber's book garnered moderate scholarly praise and a bit of public attention. But he exploded into the public limelight during the 1972 presidential campaign after he wrote a few short paragraphs about how a reelected Richard Nixon might behave. Reviewing Nixon's pre-presidency life and evidence from his first term, Barber wrote of Nixon's character, pointing to "its themes of power and control, its declaration of independence, its self-concern, its damning of doubters, and its coupling of humiliation with defeat." Barber saw significant risk in reelecting Nixon: "This character could lead the president on to disaster. . . . The danger is that crisis will be transformed into tragedy . . . when and if Nixon is confronted with a severe threat to his power and sense of virtue."[42]

Did Barber predict the Watergate scandal? Not exactly, but he had worked from his theory of presidential character, mixed it with the available evidence, and provided a compelling interpretation of the Nixon presidency. Adherents to the rational choice approach, in this instance at least, could not make a similar claim.

The bundle of intertextual relations comprising the character discourse has been excavated here as a set of unresolved tensions: within the news media on the relationship between private misdeeds and the public interest, and between the unrealism of *Scandal* and the equal unrealism of the scientific-rational approach. Politicians are not, as *Scandal* would have it, each and all murderous villains. Yet is the political science construction—that politicians are pure rational advantage seekers without inner, contradictory drives—any more realistic than this deliberately dippy TV portrayal?

These tensions should not mask the shared meanings that circulate within this discourse. In fiction and in political science, elites in Washington, DC, are portrayed as cynical game players, deceptive and mostly effective in hiding their lies from public view. However unrealistic in its details *Scandal* may be, this interpretation of politics reflects a broadly taken-for-granted cultural belief about our public figures.

Have we created for ourselves the worst of all worlds? Our fictions and our journalism circulate wild speculations about the unconstrained passions of our political figures, forcing them into ever deeper defensive crouches. They portray implausibly perfect public selves that read false to every citizen with a halfway functional bullshit detector. Our political science endorses the view that the political elite are rampant advantage seekers but offers such a thin account of their motivations that we are left without a useful framework for spotting the truly dangerous personality amid the morass of human foible.

Gary Hart lamented the situation. He accused the media of treating him like "some kind of rare bird, some extraordinary creature that has to be dissected by those who analyze politics to find out what makes him tick." Hart said this "reduces the press of this nation to hunters and presidential candidates to being hunted." After Hart crashed out of the 1988 race, former president Richard Nixon wrote a fan letter to the Colorado senator:

> Dear Gary: This is just a line to tell you that I thought you handled a difficult situation uncommonly well. . . . What you said about the media needed to be said. They demand the right to ruthlessly question the ethics of everyone else. But when anyone else dares to question their ethics, they hide behind the shield of freedom of speech. They refuse to make the distinction that philosophers throughout the centuries have made between freedom and license. [43]

After reporter Paul Taylor had asked Gary Hart "the adultery question," a reader sent a letter to his paper: "To have destroyed Richard Nixon, I applauded you. For what you did to Gary Hart, I damn you all to hell, and for those of you who aren't saints, I pray your dicks fall off."[44]

5 | Compromise—*Borgen*

The quintessential American board game is *Monopoly*. Players race to buy up property, charge rent to those who set foot upon it, and try to drive the other players into bankruptcy. The goal is individual wealth creation. The equivalent in Denmark is called *Konsensus*.[1] Each player tries to put themselves into the mind-set of the others in order to give the same answers to common questions. The game is won by empathizing with the other players, not ruining them.

Like its gaming culture, Danish political culture is very different from adversarial American democracy. Danish politics is about coalition building among a multiplicity of parties, operating in a parliament where no one party has an overall majority. The government is much larger than in the US, and cradle-to-grave welfare provisions make it venerated, not despised. This in spite of the highest taxation rates in the world.

Danish politics is about debate embedded within consensus. Difficult problems are approached from a common basis of facts and commitment to process and to a myth of "Danishness" perpetuated by the cultural, educational, and political apparatus of the state and civil society.[2]

Borgen, the first televised dramatization of Danish politics, takes our argument beyond the adversarial and zero-sum political culture in the United States, a culture that is reflected and refracted in the political fictions and political science we have examined so far. Danish political culture generates a politics of compromise, one that involves the negotiation of conflict rather than its absence.

"We were told to really lower our expectations when it came to an international audience for the series," says Adam Price, the creator of *Borgen*. "Probably Sweden and Norway [nations with similar political systems and cultures] would take it out of politeness, but that would be it."[3]

Price was wrong. *Borgen* became an international hit. The series' interpretation of politics gained adherents among the cultural intelligentsia first in the UK and later in the US. The show was appointment viewing for the British prime minister and leader of the opposition. The French president was a fan, too, and Hillary Clinton wrote a note of appreciation to the producers.[4] Series star Sidse Babett Knudsen, who played Prime Minister Birgitte Nyborg, was amazed at the reception: "It never occurred to me that this series would travel abroad," she says. "I mean, it's about Danish coalition politics." Moreover, it is subtitled from a language, Danish, that Knudsen describes as resoundingly unappealing: "It sounds like you are throwing up."[5]

The fiction speaks an alien political language as well. *Borgen* shows a vivid politics characterized by difficult decisions made by competent and mature adults amid a setting of stylish informality. This difference from the adversarial, gridlocked, partisan American democracy made it an object of fascination. The discourse of compromise was an attractive alternative to the failed persuasion, rampant ambition, and sordid plumbing of character deficiencies we have examined in the last few chapters.

Audiences decoded *Borgen* by way of other screen fictions, particularly *The West Wing*. Both Price, the show's creator, and Jeppe Gjervig Gram, one of the writers, acknowledge Sorkin's show as an influence. Price embraced the idealism of *The West Wing*. "I wanted to salute democracy," he says. "I didn't want to write a show where all of the politicians are devious dirty bastards constantly trying to sugar their own cake."[6] Gram talks giddily about the American show: "*The West Wing* is my favourite show. To me it's up there with the big works of the last century: Seriously: it's the Bible. It's Shakespeare."[7]

But Price insists *Borgen* is not just *The West Wing-in-Denmark*. Whereas the Aaron Sorkin show focused on the staffers surrounding the president, and gave us a clear home team to root for, *Borgen* is much more about the good faith, intelligent cut-and-thrust that characterizes the collaborative and fact-based Danish political system, where more than one side has a fair argument and politics is not about winning and losing but about reconciling sincerely held views within a system based on trust and negotiation. "The West Wing is about a football team all playing for the president," Price says. "Borgen is about characters standing on each column of modern democracy and actually working against each other. . . . I'm a big fan of The West Wing, but I truly believe this series is quite different."[8] *Borgen*'s politicians work in good faith, but "they are sometimes forced into very, very difficult choices."[9] Where *The West Wing* was about elite persuasion, *Borgen* is about compromise.

One reference point, then, is *The West Wing*. In order to flesh out the language of *compromise*, and add it to our political lexicon, it is necessary to further set *Borgen* in context. The institutional structure of Danish politics must be elaborated. More than this, though, it is crucial to understand the historical and cultural circumstances that surround this structure. While political science research on the dynamics of multiparty systems is useful in interpreting *Borgen*, this televised fiction prompts an inquiry into how these structures develop and operate in specific national contexts. Danish political culture, made meaningful to us through *Borgen*, indicates that hopes for the *Borgenization* of American politics are futile. The culture that makes political compromise possible in Denmark cannot be recreated elsewhere by merely copying its political institutions.

A Primer on Danish Politics

Borgen is set among the Copenhagen power elite. To understand the show, we need to understand Danish politics. Denmark has a prime ministerial executive, a coalition-based legislature, and a multi-member, proportional representation electoral system.

Although Denmark has many parties covering an array of ideological positions, the party system exhibits strong centripetal tendencies. In other words, the fight in Danish politics is for the center ground, not the polarized extremes.[10] The Danish *Folketing*, or Parliament, currently has 13 parties represented among its 179 members. The Social Democrats and *Venstre* (liberals) are traditionally the largest. No single party has had an overall majority in the Folketing since 1909. Danish government is government by coalition, with multiple parties forming an alliance in the Parliament.

Unusually for coalition-based systems, alliances in the Folketing rarely achieve an overall majority, and this is not seen as a big problem. Since 1945 only four coalitions have commanded a stable majority in Parliament. Most of the time, minority coalitions make bill-by-bill deals with the other parties.

Formal institutions are only part of the story of Danish government, though. More important is the culture of negotiation and agreement. The crucial ingredients are a common sense of purpose with regard to the big national challenges along with solidarity across class lines in this fundamentally homogenous society.[11]

Danish political scholars see their system as unique, a "negotiational democracy."[12] Hjalte Rasmussen writes of a "truly pervasive emphasis on politicians' agreements," drawing a stark contrast with the zero-sum political culture of the United States. Rasmussen analogizes Denmark to a well-run corporation, with a unionized workforce heavily involved in the governance of the country.

The ideological conflicts that rend other countries are fused in a sort of Danish national political idea, "a typically Danish melting pot that submerged the dominant influence or taste of any single ingredient." The national political idea borrows elements of socialism, liberalism, and populism. "The hallmark," Rasmussen concludes, is the belief "that legislation and other public policies ought to emerge and be given life and blood [through] debate among independent and well-meaning people—and never social classes."[13]

Denmark confounds the fears of some about consensus politics and government by coalition—that it must be weak and cautious.[14] The traditional argument against proportional representation is that it produces stalemate, as no party has enough power to enact its agenda. Yet Danish politics is vibrant and progressive, and citizens trust the government significantly more than people do in the US. They also turn out to vote in much higher numbers—usually around 85 percent.

The comprehensive welfare state is the central legislative achievement of this national consensus. More than a set of laws and programs, it is, in the words of the author of the best one-volume history on Denmark, "a philosophy of life."[15] Danes receive free (at the point of access) health care and university education. And Danes laid off from their jobs can expect to receive unemployment benefits from the state almost equaling the lost salary beginning the day they are made redundant and lasting for up to four years. This is paid for with astonishingly high rates of income tax—50 percent on average.

Yet perhaps even more important is the Danish economic model, a seemingly paradoxical combination of free-trade capitalism with a level of social welfare more usually associated with socialism. The system is known as "flexicurity" and represents a mutually beneficial compromise between employers and workers.[16] Denmark imposes few restrictions on the rights of employers to lay workers off. A little advance notice is required, but other than that a Danish business can sack an employee more or less whenever they choose. This gives business the flexibility to not only shed costs in a downturn and hire quickly in an upturn but also refresh their workforce with motivated employees with up-to-the-minute skills.

With significant unemployment benefits, losing a job doesn't mean losing an income. And unemployed workers are offered training to reenter the workforce with additional skills or, if they choose, switch careers entirely and learn another profession at the state's expense.[17] Danes change jobs frequently: one in three does so every year, and 70 percent believe frequent changes are a good idea.[18] Doing so is made easier by a comparatively equal wage structure. The pay gap between a manufacturing job and a service-sector job is tiny, and even between a lawyer and a refuse collector the difference in earnings is much less than in the US. Only 4 percent of Danes live below the poverty line.[19]

How did Denmark come to have this political-economic system? Does it produce compromise politics, or is it a reflection of a wider compromise culture? An examination of Danish political history may clarify.

How Denmark Got Its Consensus Politics

Denmark is a small country of 5.5 million people yet was once a large empire, encompassing Norway and the now German provinces of Schleswig and Holstein. The story of Denmark gaining its consensus politics is revealed to be, on closer examination, the story of Denmark losing its empire.

Imperial Denmark, a multiethnic state, was a significant geopolitical force. Like Great Britain, it relied on a powerful fleet to protect its trading interests. In the eighteenth century, Denmark was one of the most militarized states in Europe and was allied with Napoleon in the wars of the era. Denmark suffered a decisive defeat in 1813. The Danish fleet was sunk by the British Royal Navy, so the power base for the empire was lost. Norway became independent, and Denmark would never again be a global power.

Yet amid this defeat, the Napoleonic era brought significant progressive reforms. In 1788 the Danish king Christian VII faced turmoil as peasants rebelled against the law of adscription, a dictate forbidding them from leaving the region of their birth. Adscription rendered the majority of Danish farmers and laborers as serfs of the local nobles, who benefited from the guaranteed supply of cheap labor.

In France and the United States in these years, the arbitrary dictates of absolutist monarchs were overcome through violent rebellion, and a tradition of suspicion of state power was born. In Denmark, King Christian VII simply abolished adscription, and the rest of the elite quietly implemented his wishes. The king and, by extension, the state came to be seen as champions of the freedom of the people rather than its repressors.[20]

Although shorn of Norway, Denmark was still multicultural at this point, with a sizable German population in the southern provinces of Schleswig and Holstein. Yet once the German chancellor Otto Von Bismarck started to unify the Prussian states, it was only a matter of time before Denmark's powerful neighbor claimed the two territories.

Dismembered Denmark lost two-thirds of its land mass and one-third of its population. Danes now knew that theirs was a vulnerable state with powerful neighbors. Not only were the days of empire over, but the survival of an independent Denmark was in doubt. This sense of vulnerability was heightened in the twentieth century by the Nazi occupation of Denmark and the presence of an aggressive Soviet Union to the east.

What was left after the losses of the eighteenth and nineteenth centuries was a small state but one with an unusually homogenous population. The congruence of ethnicity and territory in Denmark was almost perfect.[21] The opportunity was, in the words of a popular nineteenth-century Danish slogan, to "make up for outward losses with internal gains."[22] A culture of Danishness was consciously constructed, one that emphasized the solidarity of the Danish national family. This was a gentle nationalism, of mutual nurturing and a duty of care.

The key figure was the poet and priest N.F.S. Grundtvig.[23] Somewhere between a Danish Jefferson and Lincoln, Grundtvig married his love for Denmark with prodigious literary and organizational skills to shape a national idea. He recast the losses of territory and population as strengths. Danes were one people, each of equal worth, tightly bound together into a nation that would draw strength from unity.

> Far whiter mountains shine splendidly forth
> Than the hills of our native islands
> But we Danish rejoice in the quiet North
> For our lowlands and rolling highlands
> No towering peaks thundered over our birth
> It suits us best to remain on earth.

Other states would be powerful players in global politics. Other states would be riven by divisions between social classes, between economic interests, and between the people and the government. Danes, though, would be a grounded people, working quietly and in unison. Wealth was to be found, Grundtvig wrote, not in the construction of great industrial capacity, the acquisition of a vast empire, or the accumulation of capital, but in the perfection of the Danish union. "When few have too much and fewer too little then truly we have become wealthy."[24] Grundtvig and his followers established a network of church and educational institutions to spread his ideas, which remain the foundation of the national culture.

In the United States the size and scope of national government is a source of partisan division. The founding idea of America—a rebellion against government power—has embedded a deep distrust of the motives and capacity of government to administer big programs. The American ideology of individualism rests on a belief that achievements are the product of hard work and personal virtue. So redistribution of wealth via government is generally viewed with suspicion.

But Danish history has created a different context for the state. The government is seen as a partner and an enabler of the aspirations of the people. Society is much less class conscious and, with its small size and ethnic homogeneity, more akin to a family. As a consequence, the Danish state, and the governing class as a whole, is a source of pride rather than partisan angst.

Borgen

If Danish politics is a utopia of state-provided opulence and negotiated agreement, shouldn't *Borgen*, as a dramatization of its power elite, be a bit boring? Far from it. Adam Price, the creator and main writer of *Borgen*, highlights the challenges facing modern Denmark and reminds us that compromise is the navigation of conflict, not its absence.

The first shot of the series is a quotation from Italian philosopher Niccolo Machiavelli, the master of political maneuver. "A prince should have no other aim or thought but war and its organization and discipline." *Borgen* begins with a very Danish political war, one fought over the center ground. It is three days before a national election, and the prime minister, Lars Hesselboe of the Liberal Party, is defending his government, a coalition with the right-wing Freedom Party. The opposition coalition is headed by the cynical Michael Laugesen of Labour. His junior partner is Birgitte Nyborg of the Moderates.

Nyborg, played by Sidse Babbett Knudsen, is the series protagonist. She has negotiated a deal with her stay-at-home husband—five years for her career, five years for his—but still worries that she doesn't see her kids enough and that the pastries provided at the endless meetings at Parliament (political compromise in action) have caused her to gain weight. "The dry cleaner shrunk it," her husband assures her when she can't fit into her favorite skirt.

She also has a deal with her coalition partner, Labour's Laugesen, about their joint platform for the election: they will follow a tolerant policy toward asylum seekers in Denmark. But Laugesen is an opportunist, and on TV he makes a play for right-wing voters: he reneges on the deal. Nyborg is blindsided. "Can you still support Laugesen?" the TV host asks. Her spin doctor motions frantically through the studio glass that she should say yes. It is the rational political move. The Laugesen-Nyborg coalition is leading in the polls, and on the precipice of government. "No. If that is Labour's policy, I cannot support them."

The opposition coalition is fractured, but the incumbent liberals are in a worse position. Prime Minister Hesselboe is embroiled in a corruption scandal—albeit a genteel, Danish scandal: the flustered prime minister had mistakenly used a government credit card to make a small personal purchase. When Laugesen tries to exploit the mini-scandal in the final preelection debate, Hesselboe is wounded, but Laugesen's aggressive attack rebounds and damages the opposition leader too.

Desperate, Laugesen offers Nyborg a new deal: extra seats in the post-election cabinet in return for accepting his intolerant line on refugees. But Laugesen is an ugly man, all leering looks and straying hands around his female colleagues. He tries his mediocre charm on Nyborg: "Birgitte! You've been on my mind the past few days. Sounds like the story of a great romance!" She looks at him with disdain. "I understand your interest in a marriage of convenience, but I'm an old-fashioned girl. My answer is no."

Laugesen's attack on Hesselboe was electoral murder-suicide, and Nyborg's Moderate Party gains an unprecedented fifteen seats. The queen asks her to form a government. She goes home to her husband. "They want me for prime minister."

Making Meaning of *Borgen* through Political Science

Danish governments are formed by postelection negotiations among the party leaders. Birgitte is appointed "Royal Investigator" and serves as the chairperson of negotiations to form a new government. These are episodes of strategic interplay among the political elite, where one party's best move depends on the moves made by all the others. They are rife for analysis by the rational choice paradigm in political science, although the expectations of cynical, zero-sum maneuverings collide here with a positive-sum, compromise political culture.

Parties in coalition systems often form preelection alliances, such as the Laugesen-Nyborg pact, to give voters a sense of what they are voting for. When that alliance fractures or the election outcome is unclear, as in the first episode of *Borgen*, postelection negotiations take place. Political scientists have developed a number of ways to model these negotiations.[25] Each begins with an assumption about what the parties really want. The most straightforward assumption is that rational politicians simply want to achieve power. In this instance, they are expected to make the deal that grants them the highest likelihood of taking the most senior office available.

William H. Riker is the central political science figure in this "theory of coalitions."[26] Riker argued that rational politicians will form a coalition that is just sufficient to take power and no larger. This "minimum winning coalition" is logical, Riker wrote: you need an alliance big enough to win, but you also want to maximize the proportion of that alliance made up by your own party. If you control fifty seats, it is better to have a winning coalition of one hundred than of two hundred, as your share in the former is 50 percent but only 25 percent in the latter. Why dilute your own influence?

In practice, though, minimum winning coalitions are far less common than Riker predicted. Political scientists explain this by introducing other factors that are posited to influence coalition negotiations.[27] In some instances a new government might want to maximize rather than minimize its size. Winston Churchill did this in the usually coalition-averse British Parliament during the Second World War. The goal was national unity under threat of Nazi invasion rather than partisan advantage under politics as usual. In less fraught times it might still make sense to have as large a majority as possible. Major policy initiatives might require supermajorities—say a two-thirds vote—so bigger is better.

Politicians may pursue goals beyond the mere acquisition of power. It can be rational to pursue ideological and policy goals too.[28] Anthony Downs came up with a simple yet powerful model of ideology and coalitions.[29] He relied on an analogy, developed by the economist Harold Hotelling, showing how businesses respond to market competition. Hotelling imagined a street with one hundred equally spaced houses: where would two small business owners place their stores in order to attract the most customers from the residents of the street? To best serve their customers, the first store owner would place her business between the twenty-fourth and twenty-fifth houses, and the second would place his between the seventy-fourth and seventy-fifth houses. That way no resident would have to walk farther than twenty-five houses to reach one of the stores. Yet the store owners are in competition for customers. Therefore, the first owner places her store between the forty-ninth and fiftieth houses (ensuring everyone from house one to forty-nine uses her store), and the second owner places his between the fiftieth and fifty-first houses (capturing the business of residents fifty-one through one hundred.)

Downs applied this creative thinking to politics. Instead of a street with houses, he posited a continuum of ideological competition with voters preferring certain points on that continuum. Downs argued that the key source of competition in politics is over basic economic policies, with the left favoring state ownership and regulation and the right favoring the free market. Like store owners, party leaders want to maximize their share of the available business and thus place their party at the point on the continuum where they can capture the most votes.

In a system like that of the US or the UK, with few parties and an electoral system that usually produces a single-party majority, Downs imagined that party leaders would behave like Hotelling's store owners and gravitate toward the center ground. In a proportional representation system like Denmark, though, political parties can get some measure of power with even quite small vote totals, so it is rational for them to seek out a distinctive niche on the ideological spectrum and then bargain their way into office in coalition with other parties.[30]

A party of the left prefers to go into government with other parties of the left, or at least the center, rather than make an uncomfortable alliance with a noncompatible party of the right. Even if politicians are willing to make ideologically irrational alliances, they know that the resulting government will be unstable and that voters will punish them at the next election.

This combination of size and ideological positioning determines the bargaining leverage a party will have in coalition negotiations. Larger parties, of course, have more leverage, but even small parties can be crucial if they have the final few seats necessary to cross the tipping point and create a government. All else being equal, parties in the ideological center have more leverage, because they are ideologically compatible with a greater number of partners.

How would Downs, a prominent political scientist in the scientific-rational school, interpret the coalition bargaining in *Borgen*? Birgitte Nyborg's Moderates are only the third-biggest party—they doubled their parliamentary numbers in the election—but Labour and the incumbent Liberals still have more seats. Nyborg begins negotiations logically, meeting with all parties in the Folketing and refusing to rule out any coalition: "This is a new government. Everyone gets a chance."

Nyborg occupies what Anthony Downs would consider excellent territory: her Moderate Party bestrides the center ground of the Danish ideological spectrum. To her left, starting with the most extreme, are:

- The Solidarity Party: quasi-revolutionaries led by Anne Sophie Lindenkrone, a former radical activist. A small party.
- The Greens: a party focused on ecological conservation led by Amir Diwan. Also a small party.
- Labour: a large center-left party, the analog to the real-world Danish Social Democrats who were in office (as part of various coalitions) for much of the twentieth century. Labour are led by Michael Laugesen until his election-eve implosion, and Bjørn Marrot, a stolid figure, afterward. Labour are the largest party after the election.

To Nyborg's ideological right are:

- The Liberals: in office as the series begins, led by Prime Minister Lars Hesselboe. They are the analog to the real-world Venstre Party, traditionally the competitor to the Social Democrats for largest party. In the *Borgen* election, the Liberals win the second-highest number of seats, but their coalition loses its majority and, after the credit card scandal, Hesselboe has lost his credibility as prime minister.
- The New Conservatives: a small party, hawkish on defense issues, led by Yvonne Kjaer.
- The Freedom Party: farthest to the right. The Freedom Party advocates an end to immigration, especially by Muslims, and a return to what they see as traditional Danish cultural values. An analog to the real-world Danish People's Party, a consistent force with about 10–15 percent of the vote in Danish elections. Led, in the show, by Svend Åge Saltum.

The logical coalition is with Labour, and with Laugesen crippled by his poor election performance, it seems that Birgitte can negotiate a good deal with the weakened party. Laugesen may not survive as party leader, and Birgitte offers Labour a coalition with her at its head. But Laugesen blows off the meeting, only to return a day later to offer Nyborg a junior post. He, Laugesen, would be prime minister.

Nyborg refuses, and the arrogant Laugesen is toppled as Labour leader.

Meanwhile, incumbent Liberal Party prime minister Lars Hesselboe makes Birgitte a counteroffer. He will stay as prime minister and Nyborg's Moderates will hold five ministries in a center/right coalition.

Birgitte goes back to Labour and the Green Party with the Hesselboe offer as leverage. I'm going into government with the Liberals, she tells them, unless we agree on a center/left coalition right now, with Nyborg as prime minister. With the deal in hand, she confronts a complacent Hesselboe, who assumes his offer cannot be matched: "Lars, we have to let you down. We want someone else as prime minister." "Who?" he asks. "Me."

Nyborg's new government, a Moderate-Labour-Green-Solidarity coalition with a young cabinet that is 50 percent female, marches triumphantly to the front of the Parliament building to greet the press. Birgitte, her face scrunched up in pure joy, waves to the crowd as Denmark's new *Staatsminister*.

Down's theories significantly enhance our understanding of *Borgen*'s coalition negotiations—this fiction from political science adds to our understanding of the screen fiction. It showcases the heuristic power of the scientific-rational paradigm to isolate the logic of many political decisions.

In *Borgen* these rational negotiations take place within a compromise political culture. The goal is to provide a moderate government and to govern the country rather than to seize political power at whatever cost and destroy or marginalize all opposition. My argument throughout this book has been that the scientific-rational approach in US political science is a useful fiction but not a value-free reflection of fact. This useful fiction should not be the taken-for-granted, it-must-be-this-way background for politics. An assumption of rationality need not become an assumption of cynicism and self-interest in our politics. The cultural principles that underpin and construct rationality vary by time and place, and if they support compromise, then, as in *Borgen*, strategic politicians can act for the public good.

Leadership as compromise

Once in government, Birgitte must marry strategic considerations to a more complex set of circumstances. In so doing, she gives perhaps the most believable portrayal of a decent, extremely competent public figure on political television. She is in utter command of the issues, but the writers do not give her the showy verbosity of a Jed Bartlet. She is a formidable political strategist but does not resort to the low cunning of a Frank Underwood. She is far from the narrowly drawn, insular member of the political elite imagined by the political fictions and political science we have discussed so far.

Instead, we have a progressive and collegial politician seeking cross-party agreement in the best Danish tradition. Nyborg has the self-confidence to accept challenges without needing to crush those who disagree with her. Yet she is never cowed; when the male heads of the Danish intelligence agencies are reluctant to read her in on state secrets, she snaps at them, "Don't play your gentleman's club games with me." Although her opponents sometimes criticize her for softheaded liberalism, she at times displays the face-to-face toughness of a Tony Soprano, as her traitorous minister Troels Höxenhaven discovers when he crosses her: "You are a dead man in my government."[31]

Yet Nyborg is far from a superhero, and her utter devotion to the office of prime minister causes profound damage to her family life. A theme of *Borgen* is that the political class is an exception to the vaunted Danish achievement of work/life balance, as few political figures are able to square a happy family life with the demands—and the allure—of Parliament. As Bent Sejrø, Birgitte's great ally, sighs, "We are great at compromising at work but useless at it at home." *Borgen* creator Adam Price wanted to weave this struggle between public and private life throughout the show. He came to realize that the core question he was asking was "Can you be in power and remain yourself?"[32]

Birgitte's husband, Philip Christensen, is a talented businessman, and their relationship is based on a delicate trade-off: Birgitte's political career will take precedence for five years, while Philip stays at home with their two children, and then Philip will return to work while Birgitte takes an extended sabbatical. Yet Birgitte becomes prime minister as her five years are coming to a close, and the bargain collapses. She is rarely at home, Philip becomes increasingly frustrated and eventually seeks a divorce, while their two children succumb to anxiety-related illnesses. It's a profoundly sad dramatization of the cost of a high-level political career. As Denmark's first female prime minister, Birgitte faces a dilemma common to highly accomplished women: when both work and home demand total attention, does something have to give?

The show is too smart, though, to have Birgitte become a sainted and tragic feminist icon. She is instead a fully drawn human being with many talents and flaws. She gets drunk one night and has sex with her young driver. The next morning, she has him fired. She admits to Sejrø that, while she knows she should prioritize her ailing home life, she works ever longer hours at the office: "I'm happier working and not having to deal with my family."

Price wanted to avoid writing a show with a clichéd "strong female character." Instead, Nyborg is a composite of strength with frailty, workplace achievement, and home-life catastrophe. "I wanted her to become a very, very good politician," he said, "but a very bad wife, a very distracted mother, because this job is so incredibly demanding." Premium television in the era of *Borgen* was full of nuanced male characters who fit this mold—Don Draper, Tony Soprano, Walter White—but Price felt that heroines had been portrayed with fewer contradictions. "You could argue that men have had ten thousand years of letting down their wives and their family, because they needed to lead armies into war and so on," Price reasons. "Women have only had about 100 years of professional life, and perhaps only forty, fifty years of playing a serious part in political life. Therefore I thought it would be more interesting to watch a women let down [her family] than watch a man doing the same thing we've always known them to do."[33]

Challenges

Birgitte's struggles are one of the ways *Borgen* portrays compromise. Danes are proud of their achievements in building a superb welfare state and of their trust and social cohesion. Yet, in *Borgen* and in real life, both are under threat. *Borgen* is encoded with the real-world contemporary challenges to Denmark, and for a full decoding, international audiences require some background.

Welfare state

The great era of the welfare state in highly developed countries was the half century after the Second World War. Progressive governments built systems of education, medical care, pensions, and unemployment relief that, in the term of political scientist Gosta Esping-Andersen, "decommodified" human beings. Instead of having rights only in so far as their labor was valued in the marketplace, Esping-Andersen argues, post-1945 welfare states granted rights by virtue of citizenship. The Danish system provided for de-commodification, allowing citizens to receive education, health care, and wages even where they could not offer their labor in return.[34]

Welfare states are redistributive. Highly productive workers contribute to the system through taxation, and less productive citizens receive benefits. Across the course of a citizen's life, more is contributed during the productive years, and more is received during times of sickness, unemployment, and at the beginning and end of life. As with all welfare states, the Danish system relies on there being a critical mass of contributors to support beneficiaries.

A globalized world is a threat to an extensive welfare state model.[35] When goods, services, and people can move freely across borders, net contributors to a welfare state have an incentive to relocate to another country with lower taxes. This point is demonstrated rather vividly in *Borgen* when Birgitte has to plead with businessman Jacob Kruse, who is threatening to move his giant corporation abroad in order to avoid her government's new regulations. Kruse cannot be ignored: his business makes up 11 percent of Denmark's GDP.

The graying of the population is a further threat. In a great irony, the success of welfare states in increasing life expectancy through improvements in medical care and working conditions undermines their foundations: an older population requires more expensive late-life treatment and shifts the balance of makers and takers in favor of the latter.

Further, there is a danger that comfortable welfare state provision combined with high taxation deadens the motivation of citizens—a critique of welfare states that is prevalent in the United States and increasingly on the minds of Danes. Why work, after all, if the gap between rich, poor, and unemployed is comparatively small and welfare benefits are readily available. Karen Hækkerup, a former minister of social affairs and integration, laments, "My grandmother was offered a pension and she was offended. She did not need it. But now people do not have that mentality. They think of these benefits as their rights. The rights have just expanded and expanded. And it has brought us a good quality of life. But now we need to go back to the rights and the duties. We all have to contribute."[36]

There are painful choices to be made, then, about the level of welfare state provision that is sustainable in a globalized, graying economy. Denmark faced this with welfare reforms in the mid-1990s, ensuring that unemployment benefits were bridging payments to those actively seeking work rather than permanent incomes for the indolent. The benefits were still ample and were combined with extensive retraining programs to make sure that job seekers had the skills to contribute to the labor market. But it was made clear that receiving benefits meant accepting an obligation to seek work.[37]

Birgitte Nyborg makes welfare reform a central part of her government, trying to safeguard the state finances by ending the practice of early retirement. This leads her into conflict with her coalition partners in the Labour Party, who rely on trade union support. Unions commonly trade wage increases for deferred benefits—such as early retirement—in negotiations with employers and with government. When the unions give up wages and the government later refuses to keep its end of the bargain, conflict is inevitable.

Birgitte is at odds with Bjørn Marrot, the leader of Labour and an old trade unionist. There is pathos in the eventual defeat of Marrot, a man from another era who comes to realize that he is "the last worker." Birgitte, following the Danish political tradition of seeking to govern from the center, passes her welfare bill with votes from the right-wing opposition. She could ram through a bill with just her center-left coalition partners but asks, "Is it fair to pass something with a two-vote majority?" (Try to imagine this line spoken by a politician in *House of Cards*, *Scandal*, or even *The West Wing*.) Her point is that major national issues should be dealt with by cross-party compromise and that the kind of zero-sum partisanship that characterizes modern American politics leads to illegitimate outcomes. Still, nothing is costless, and Birgitte's shining achievement of welfare reform sets in motion events that bring about the downfall of her government.

Immigration

The challenge of immigration, especially the influx of refugees from modern wars and humanitarian crises, is an inciting force in modern Western politics. It is an especially challenging issue for Denmark. Danes' self-image rests upon their cultural unity. "What has been lost without must be made up within" became the rationale for their exceptional culture of national solidarity and trust in government. But the influx of immigrants, the majority of whom come from the Islamic world, leads to diversity in cultural beliefs and norms and has forced Danes to confront a painful question: are they trusting and generous people on the grounds of universal principle, or trusting and generous only toward those who look and think like themselves?[38]

The diversity question looks different in a country like the United States, founded by immigrants, and with an individualistic ethos that venerates achievement and an economic system that, at least in principle, distributes rewards by talent and work ethic. Reflecting this, the level of US taxation and welfare state provision is substantially lower than that of

Denmark. Yet even in the US, the presence of immigrants perceived to be receiving benefits is a source of huge resentment. For Danes, less accustomed to diversity and with more generous welfare benefits, the problem is more acute.

The Danish "flexicurity" labor market requires that all workers have the skills and versatility to repeatedly change jobs and shift into different sectors of the economy. The system is not designed to cope with large numbers of immigrants with shaky language skills and lower levels of education. As the editor of the Danish newspaper *Politken* wrote, "The first step of the ladder into the labor market is very steep, demanding a high level of qualifications while offering generous salaries and good working conditions." The system works well for highly skilled Danes, "but it fails in those segments of the population [such as poorly integrated immigrants] not capable of meeting the high standards—whether for social reasons or because of lack of language and other skills."[39] Embedded in a culture of trust, the system is not designed to cope with perceived shirking and benefit tourism (moving to a country specifically to take advantage of welfare state benefits). These are challenges even for the less generous, more suspicious Anglo-American welfare states.

Danes have had to wrestle with both the practical and the cultural facts of immigration. The material problem—refugees and immigrants permanently settling in Denmark and accessing the welfare state without providing commensurate labor market contributions—is exacerbated by cultural clashes. In a pattern common to European countries, immigrants and refugees from the Islamic world are portrayed by far-right parties as disproportionately prone to violence and crime. Membership of the European Union, with its open internal borders, adds another layer of tension.

In response, Danes have compromised their absolute commitment to tolerance, adopting strict immigration laws and restricting access to welfare benefits. In 2015 benefits to refugees and immigrants were cut by 45 percent. The new restrictions were so severe that *The Atlantic* magazine called Denmark "Western Europe's least attractive country for refugees."[40]

The *Dansk Folkeparti* (Danish People's Party) is the political manifestation of this tension. The DPP is nationalist and traditionalist. At the canteen in Christiansborg, their MPs refuse to eat anything other than Danish cuisine. Trine Hahnemann ran the restaurant for seven years. "If we had a tandoori on the menu or something international," he said, "there'd be a no show at lunchtime from the whole Folkeparti. Each political party also had weekly meetings where they'd have supper sent up to them and the Dansk Folkeparti ordered the same thing every week."[41]

The DPP's traditionalism extends beyond the lunchtime menu. The party yearns for a return to the ethnic homogeneity of a Denmark comprised solely of Danes. They claim to be the real guardians of the welfare state, arguing that this prized Danish achievement cannot survive in a multicultural state.[42]

In *Borgen* the Freedom Party led by the rustic Svend Åge Saltum is the fictional analog to the DPP. Svend Åge's anti-immigrant politics set him on a collision course with Nyborg. Saltum challenges her in a televised debate. "What do these people in their flowing robes want in the Danish suburbs? They come here from far away and let their offspring roam the Danish streets flashing knives." Birgitte answers, "We are the twelfth-richest country in the world. These are people in need."

Yet Svend Åge plays the trump card of N.F.S. Grundtvig, the bard of modern Danish nation building. Denmark should remember that its strength comes from its internal cohesion and that as a small state, little Denmark can't make a difference in the world and should not involve itself in global problems. Saltum ends with one of Grundtvig's most famous lines: "Our lot is not that of grandeur and gale. Let us stay close to the ground, from whence we hail."

Compromise

Borgen reminds us of the oldest political truth: that everything comes with a price, and one can rarely have the upsides of a political system or policy without, at some point, confronting its downsides. The Danish system, and the model of consensus politics and social democratic welfare capitalism within which it broadly fits, has huge advantages. The country is rich and happy, and its politics of agreement seem alluring when set alongside the zero-sum and often gridlocked state of, for example, the contemporary American scene. Yet, if by no means rotten, the state of Denmark is at least uncertain in the face of challenges to its welfare state model and its cultural homogeneity.

Among the interpretations of politics we have studied, *Borgen* is in some ways the exception that proves the rule: a realistic and positive vision of politics that portrays the elite as neither cold calculators nor polymath superhumans. The reaction to *Borgen* from British and American political observers was to instantly hope for the transfer of the Danish model to their system. If only our politics were more Danish, then perhaps our lives would reach Danish levels of happiness. Yet the Danish model was forged in a national experience over many hundreds of years, and its institutions are deeply embedded in that experience rather than being templates that can be lifted out of that history and replanted somewhere else. This, too, is another salutary reminder to political scientists about the dangers of context-free models of politics, of seeking simplification rather than cultural context.

Rational theories of politics contribute to the bundle of meanings we have called *compromise*. Models of coalitions and spatial democracy clarify which compromises are possible. But absent the cultural sinews of compromise, the models cannot deliver a *Borgenization* of our politics. Transferred to a political culture dominated by ambition and scandal, they would quickly become casualties in the zero-sum war of all against all.

Our fictions to this point have portrayed politics as a serious business. The following two chapters, by contrast, explore discourses of futility and of ineptitude, of irony and farce. The British have long regarded their politicians as figures of ridicule, tapping into a deep national suspicion of anyone who holds themselves to be superior to others. Politics, to the British, often seems like a silly game played by pompous narcissists who inevitably and deservedly fall flat on their faces. The major British political fictions, *Yes, Minister* and *The Thick of It*, reflect and perpetuate this interpretation.

6 | Bureaucracy—*Yes, Minister*

On January 20, 1984, British prime minister Margaret Thatcher issued an order to Jim Hacker, the minister of administrative affairs, and Sir Humphrey Appleby, that department's senior civil servant. She wanted to abolish the profession of economist. "All economists?" replied Hacker. Yes, she insisted, before turning to Sir Humphrey. "What are your degrees?" she asked the uncomfortable mandarin. "Politics and . . . er . . . , " Sir Humphrey trailed off. "Yes?" Thatcher insisted. "Economics," conceded Sir Humphrey. "Capital!" Thatcher delivered the final blow. "Then you'll know exactly where to start."[1]

Hacker and Sir Humphrey were characters from *Yes, Minister*, a British TV comedy that satirized the unhappy arranged marriage between feckless politicians and savvy bureaucrats. Thatcher, who was very much the real prime minister, loved the show and had pushed to appear in this one-off sketch at a television industry awards ceremony. She claimed she had written the script herself.

Behind the scenes, the Thatcher sketch infuriated most of the *Yes, Minister* team. Paul Eddington and Nigel Hawthorne, who played Hacker and Humphrey respectively, were no fans of hers. When Number 10 Downing Street proposed the sketch idea, the actors tried to get out of it. They telephoned Jonathan Lynn, cocreator of the series, who told them they had been personally invited and it was for them to decide whether to do it. "A mixture of nervousness and vanity eventually won the day," Eddington later recalled.[2]

Then they saw the script. "To say that it wasn't funny," Lynn recalls, "would be something of an understatement. We wondered if the Prime Minister had really found the time to sit down and write this crap, or whether her Press Secretary Bernard Ingham was the real author."[3]

Thatcher enjoyed *Yes, Minister*'s skewering of government bureaucracy. But the script Ingham wrote displayed little of the surgical skill with which Jay and Lynn dissected the rotting carcass of 1980s Britain—its failing industries; creaking infrastructure; bloated, wasteful public sector; and bemused political elite.

The sketch, portraying an aggressive prime minister (PM) purging the bureaucracy of technicians, missed the point of the show. Politicians in *Yes, Minister* were clueless and placid, like the protagonist Hacker, or absent entirely. (Until Hacker himself becomes PM, after season 4, we rarely see other ministers and never the unnamed head of government.) And Sir Humphrey, a grand archetype of Britain's permanent bureaucracy, would never have studied something so gauche as politics and economics. He was a classics man through and through.

And yet you could see why Thatcher called *Yes, Minister* her favorite show. Hacker was just the kind of soggy male politician she detested, and the civil service was a repeated target of her ire. Antony Jay, the cocreator, was a Thatcherite. But Jay's creative partner, Jonathan Lynn, was, like most of the cast, a leftist. "You can't pick your fans," Lynn said when he found out the real prime minister liked his work. Addressing the audience after the sketch was over, he thanked Margaret Thatcher for "finally taking her rightful place in the field of situation comedy." "It got the biggest laugh of my career," Lynn recalls. "The room was rocking, everybody except one person: Mrs. Thatcher. 'We are not amused,' her face plainly said."[4]

Yes, Minister makes meaning of politics as *bureaucracy*. Ideological waves crash against the rocks of the permanent machinery of government. Democratic choice is largely a myth; indeed the will of the people is viewed by the bureaucracy as a dangerous force that must be quietly subdued. The visible processes of government are largely an exercise in misdirection. The real decisions—or more commonly, non-decisions—are made by a deep state that is beyond scrutiny.[5]

In this interpretation of politics, the interests of the people are subverted not by the maliciousness of politicians but by their haplessness. The view of the elite in this fiction is even more sinister than in *House of Cards* and *Scandal*, where the theatrical malevolence is at least occasionally visible to the public. The villainy in *Yes, Minister* is perpetuated by civil servants whom the public never sees. This interpretation of politics is mirrored, as we shall see, in theories of bureaucracy in political science.

Jay and Lynn

When BBC journalist Antony Jay called Jonathan Lynn, an actor and screenwriter, with an idea for a sitcom based on the British civil service, Lynn passed. "I thought it sounded boring," he said.[6]

Jay had been thinking for some time about the clash between the permanent bureaucracy and democratically elected politicians. He had become interested in public choice economics, a school of thought that greatly influenced political science beginning in the 1970s. Public choice economists rejected the idea that government acts in the public interest. Instead, the public choice school argued, politicians and bureaucrats act in their own interests. Jay saw the germ of a comedy in these clashing interests. The conflict was absurd: both sides pretended that they acted out of pure motives while they were pursuing private interests and vanities.[7]

As a television journalist, Jay had seen firsthand how little politicians knew compared to how much they pretended to know. In the moments before and after the cameras were rolling, he "realised how much difference there was between the way politicians spoke on air—as if they were responsible for everything—and the fact that behind the scenes they were constantly turning to their Private Secretary [bureaucratic aide] and asking, 'What's the answer to this?'"[8]

Jay persisted with the idea for a show, and when he next met Lynn, he reminded him of an incident from some years past: In 1962 Frank Soskice, the opposition Labour Party's Home Affairs spokesman, had launched a campaign to abolish the death penalty in Britain. Soskice had blitzed the media with appeals to sign a petition, and half a million people did so over the next two years. Labour had won a majority in the 1964 general election, so Soskice had become the home secretary. Installed in office, he rejected his own petition. Jay and Lynn both found the matter darkly comic, and Jay concluded that something happens to politicians when they take charge of a ministry: they are enveloped by the civil service and housetrained in the way things are and must remain. This explained, Jay thought, the regularity with which politicians break campaign promises.[9]

Lynn was now intrigued, and shared with Jay an anecdote of his own. Lynn recalled that student politics at Cambridge, where he obtained his degree, had been dominated by gentlemen who were now rising stars in the British system: "The speakers [at student debates] included a number of ambitious and smug young men like Michael Howard and John Selwyn Gummer, who undoubtedly saw themselves as future members of a Tory government. Distressingly, less than twenty years later, that's who they were, and still wearing the same self-satisfied expressions as they sat on the front bench."[10]

They agreed to work up a script drawing upon these influences. From Jay, an intellectual, we have one of the clearer instances of academic theory influencing a political fiction, as he worked public choice themes into the show. His experience as a journalist was also brought to bear, because he had seen just how shallow was the knowledge base of many politicians. Lynn, a left-winger, brought from his Cambridge days a desire to pierce the smug veneer of the ambitious politician.

The structure of the show that emerged was simple. Protagonist Jim Hacker was an archetypal new minister. Vain and rash, equal parts idealistic and terrified, he was placed in a state of antagonistic interdependence with Sir Humphrey Appleby, the senior civil servant ("permanent secretary") of Hacker's department. Appleby's aim was to ensure that no challenge to the status quo could succeed. He sought to keep the minister as busy as possible on matters of no importance, to isolate him from external influence and advice, and to quietly ensure that his priorities—no significant change in policy and jealous protection of the scope and budget of the bureaucracy—were followed. Placed between the two of them was Bernard Woolley, a civil servant assigned as an aide to Hacker and consequently caught in a tug-of-war between the politician and the bureaucrat. Hacker was given control of the fictional Department of Administrative Affairs, which was tasked with administering the other administrative departments, thus adding a further layer of absurdity.[11]

Diaries of a Cabinet Minister and Your Disobedient Servant

Yes, Minister aimed to take the viewer into the secretive chambers of British government, revealing what had previously been known only to top-level politicians and civil servants. Jay and Lynn wanted to make the scripts as realistic as possible. As they did their research, they were surprised by how little they needed to alter the behavior of the political elite in order to render it ridiculous.

Both Jay and Lynn were fascinated in particular by the revelations in two recent books, one by a former cabinet minister and the other by a top civil servant. Diaries of a Cabinet Minister, by former minister of housing Richard Crossman, was published in 1974 after strenuous government attempts to prevent its release. Crossman had kept a meticulous journal of his life as head of a Whitehall department, and Jay and Lynn found within its pages much of the basis of their new show.[12]

Crossman's very first entry gave them their title. Crossman noted that the civil service was, to all outside appearances, profoundly deferential: "Yes, Minister! No, Minister! If you wish it, Minister!" The deference, though, was part of a spider's web into which Crossman had unwittingly flown. Standing sentry at the center of this web was his department's permanent secretary, Dame Evelyn Sharp. Crossman had been switched at the last minute from the education portfolio for which he had prepared. Dame Evelyn had completed a decade in her post, and Crossman, a neophyte in housing policy, would be the sixth minister with whom she had worked.

Whereas Crossman understood few of the issues with which his new department dealt, Dame Evelyn was supremely confident. "She sees the ordinary human being as incapable of making a sensible decision," Crossman wrote. She viewed her role as a daily "battle to save her department from my stupidity and ignorance." She would work on her hapless new minister, "grooming me . . . well, grooming is the wrong word because she is too tough and granite-like, but she has been watching, measuring, lecturing."

Whereas Dame Evelyn left Crossman terrified, and his lack of preparation left him confused, the rest of the bureaucracy sought to reassure him that little must (and, indeed, could) be done. Surrendering to the status quo was the only viable option. "I already realize the tremendous effort it requires not to be taken over by the civil service machine," Crossman wrote. The minister was kept isolated from all but official advice, with his office assuming in his mind the quality of a "padded cell." He was allowed few visitors, and these were carefully monitored to make sure the minister did not receive dangerous information or ideas.

Rather than requiring Crossman's informed attention, the mechanism of government operated smoothly without his lifting a finger. Dame Evelyn had the answers to the big questions, and the more prosaic responsibilities of memoranda and correspondence were easily discharged. Daunted on his first day by the volume of paperwork, Crossman asked his new private secretary how he could possibly cope. Simple, the civil servant replied: if he were to move the documents from his inbox to his outbox, without making even a mark upon them, the civil service would ensure that each piece of paper received an appropriate reply, and the minister need never see it again.

Thus did Crossman's ministerial life proceed: kept isolated, reliant on the bureaucracy for information and analysis, and encouraged at every turn to let things proceed as they had always done. Crossman was engaged in a constant losing battle to direct his ministry. *Diaries of a Cabinet Minister* was rich fodder for Jay and Lynn: "We referred constantly to it," Jay said.[13]

Crossman's book gave the politician's perspective. The view from Whitehall (a road in Central London on which many government administrative buildings are located) came in a second tell-all memoir: Leslie Chapman's *Your Disobedient Servant*. Chapman, a regional director at the Ministry of Public Buildings and Works, detailed the wastefulness in Britain's vast bureaucracy and the tactics civil servants used to inflate their budgets.

Believing he should promote the efficient use of resources, Chapman set up inspection units that would travel to government properties and examine their practices. He found that while civil servants have "many good qualities," as administrators they are "disastrous failures." Insulated from market pressure and accountability, Chapman concluded, costs spiral and efficiency plunges.[14]

Chapman found that expensive chauffeur services were used for trips that could easily be made by bus, train, or foot, with the chauffeur idling for most of the day while their civil service passenger attended to their leisurely schedule of appointments. Storage buildings into which workers rarely went were kept at a constant seventy degrees Fahrenheit. Worksites were invariably overstaffed, with many workers engaged in "general maintenance tasks" the nature of which Chapman could not discern and which, on observation, seemed mostly to consist of sitting around drinking tea.

Corruption was not the problem; civil servants genuinely believed in the importance of what they were doing and were not personally enriching themselves. The problem was a lack of efficiency and the overriding belief that "most things, if not everything, can be made better if you spend enough public money on them."[15]

Civil servants hid their inefficiency through a series of well-honed tactics. First, budgets were always based on existing expenditures rather than beginning from zero. The result was that annual spending always went up. The current level was presented as the minimum necessary baseline for operations, with any improvement or extension of services therefore requiring additional money. While budgets for individual departments should, in theory, go up and down when government changes its priorities, in practice the dynamic was one way only: newly prioritized areas received additional monies without equivalent savings being found elsewhere.[16]

This dynamic was carefully hidden from public view. Chapman found that his inquiries about spending would be stonewalled.[17] He came to expect three stages of silence: first, "dead silence; do nothing." The attention span of critics is short, the relevant bureaucrats would reason, and attention will quickly shift to something else. If the criticism persists, move to stage two, "courageous silence." Constrained by the necessity for confidentiality in sensitive matters of government, the civil service must leave the criticisms unanswered, stoically bearing unwarranted barbs in service of the greater good.

If, against all the odds, the investigation is not stymied by stage one or two, then the final option is the relaxed admission of minimal guilt. "We are not perfect, but we are willing to learn" is the line to take. The impression of reform can be given while downplaying the severity of the problem and thanking the critic for having raised it. All but the most persistent and informed adversaries will move on. Little significant change in practice need be made.

A case in point came when Chapman raised the issue of the ubiquitous use of expensive chauffeur services. Deflection was tried at first: it had always been a touchy subject, Chapman was told. There was a lot going on at the moment. Could he instead raise it at some future time?[18] When Chapman persisted, he was met with dissembling.

> If my figures were right (and on that there had to be considerable reservations) and if the surveys effected so far were typical (on which there were further reservations), then it could only mean that I had inherited an extremely badly run region (I hadn't); or that there were some special characteristics of our client department (unspecified) which made Southern Region different from the rest; or that it was something (also unspecified) to do with our geographical location. It was pointed out that we were nearer London than most, and while the precise significance of this went unexplained, it could not be disputed.[19]

Chapman's book gave Jay and Lynn insight into the tactics the bureaucracy would use to pad their budgets. It complimented Crossman's account of the caged politician.[20]

Once *Yes, Minister* was on the air, Jay and Lynn were contacted by senior politicians who were keen to slip them story ideas from inside the chambers of government. "We found that if we gave a politician lunch with a bottle or two of good claret they would tell us everything we needed to know," Lynn recalled.[21] They discovered with glee that the more senior the politician, the more indiscreet they were. As Sir Humphrey put it in a season two episode, "The ship of state is the only ship that leaks from the top."[22]

The fruit of Jay and Lynn's extensive research were scripts with a high level of verisimilitude. Kenneth Clarke, a senior minister in the Conservative governments of the 1980s and 1990s, thought they were almost too accurate: "I've always said that [*Yes, Minister*] is far too close to life to be safely shown to the public."[23]

The episodes would be structured as follows: Hacker, flushed with enthusiasm for some new idea, asserts himself. Sir Humphrey deflects and stalls, spinning a web of confusion to entrap the minister. Hacker becomes gradually more exasperated and insistent before Sir Humphrey suggests that the minister's proposal would, if followed, have negative consequences for the minister's personal political fortunes. Suddenly seeing the appeal of the status quo, Hacker blurts out that the whole thing should be forgotten. "Yes, Minister," Sir Humphrey would reply. Roll credits.

The series addressed recurrent issues of British government, tied together by the common thread of inaction and elite secrecy. It became one of the most quoted television shows in British history. Among the more telling lines are these:

On political time versus bureaucratic time:

HACKER: "A week is a long time in politics."
SIR HUMPHREY: "A year is a short time in government."[24]
HACKER: "You are more concerned with means than ends!"
SIR HUMPHREY: "There are no ends in administration, Minister, only loose ends. Administration is eternal."[25]
SIR HUMPHREY: "Diplomacy is about surviving to the next century. Politics is about surviving until next Friday."[26]

On democracy and politicians:

SIR HUMPHREY: "Ministers are appointed almost at random, by prime ministerial whim, in recognition of dubious services rendered or to avoid appointing someone of real talent."[27]
SIR HUMPHREY: "We run a civilized, aristocratic system of government, tempered only by occasional general elections."[28]
SIR HUMPHREY: "Politician's logic: Something must be done. This is something. Therefore we must do it."[29]

On the interests of the bureaucracy:

HACKER: "Political opponents are the opposition in exile. Civil servants are the opposition in residence."[30]
SIR HUMPHREY: "If we didn't fight for our budget we might end up with a department so small that even a minister could run it!"[31]

HACKER: "Three articles of civil service faith: It takes time to do things quickly, it's more expensive to do things cheaply, and it's more democratic to do things in secret."[32]

SIR HUMPHREY: "It's my job to carry out government policy."

HACKER: "Even if you think it's wrong?"

SIR HUMPHREY: "Well, almost all government policy is wrong, but frightfully well carried out."[33]

On how to manage a minister:

SIR HUMPHREY: "This country is governed by ministers making decisions from amongst the alternatives we present to them. If they had all the facts, they might see all sorts of alternatives. They might even formulate their own plans instead of choosing between the two or three we put out."[34]

SIR HUMPHREY, ON THE "CIVIL SERVANTS FOUR-WORD TRICK":

To get the minister to accept a policy, say it is "Quick. Simple. Popular. Cheap.

To get the minister to reject a policy, say it is "Complicated. Lengthy. Expensive. Controversial.

To be really sure they will reject it: "Say the decision is 'courageous.'"[35]

SIR HUMPHREY: "There is an implicit promise between the minister [and the civil service]. If he will help us by implementing the opposite policy to the one he promised in the manifesto, we will help him by making it look like he is doing exactly what he promised."[36]

After Jay and Lynn had completed four successful seasons of *Yes, Minister*, they knew they needed a change. The length of Hacker's tenure at the Department of Administrative Affairs was becoming implausible. Such was the pace of turnover in modern British government that he would have been reshuffled at least once, if not several times, over four years. With such a lengthy stay in one post, there was a danger, as Sir Humphrey might say, that he would start to know something about what his ministry did.

Instead, they did the inevitable thing with this mediocre, milquetoast minister: they had him promoted. In a one-hour special, Sir Humphrey is chosen to replace the retiring cabinet secretary as the head of the civil service. He is delighted at the prospect of escape from Hacker, his longtime antagonist. Yet the prime minister, too, decides to depart. A conclave of the most senior civil servants agrees that a suitably inert replacement must be maneuvered into the job. Hacker is the outstanding candidate.

At first glance, the episodes of *Yes, Minister* and its successor, *Yes, Prime Minister*, appear to be a series of self-contained vignettes. Yet Hacker's promotion solidified a change in the relationship between the politician and the civil servant. Something of a deer-in-the-headlights at first, Hacker had become over time a more equal antagonist and, occasionally, partner in crime to Sir Humphrey. As prime minister, Hacker develops alternative sources of information and advice and is often able to make the heretofore imperturbable Sir Humphrey sweat a little, to work a little harder to stay in control.

At one point, for example, Hacker confiscates Sir Humphrey's key to the cabinet room, where the prime minister does his work. Desperate to regain access to the inner sanctum of power, Sir Humphrey sprints about Whitehall looking for another entrance and ends up shinning his way along a Downing Street balcony and pounding on the cabinet room window, begging for entry. Hacker is, for at least a moment, a powerful prime minister.[37] How Mrs. Thatcher must have enjoyed that episode.

Bureaucracy and Rationality

Antony Jay's interest in public choice theory gave the series its intellectual heft. The perspective was prominent in both real-world politics and political science when *Yes, Minister* was conceived. The core insight was that policy makers (politicians) and policy implementers (bureaucrats) followed their private interests rather than the public good. This led them into conflict with one another.[38] The conflict takes the form of an intra-elite game, separate and mostly invisible from the non-elite.

At the forefront of the public choice movement was William A. Niskanen, a product of Milton Friedman's famous Chicago school of economic analysis. When he trained his analytical sights upon the bureaucracy, Niskanen knew of what he spoke: he had served as one of Secretary of Defense Robert McNamara's "whiz kids" in the Pentagon. McNamara believed that an analytical mind-set and strict adherence to statistical methods could improve efficiency across government and had sought Niskanen's expertise in implementing these ideas.

Niskanen, though, was disappointed by what he saw. He concluded that government was inefficient and often deceitful. Incisive in thought and tongue, Niskanen stood six foot four and spoke his mind: "I came to recognize that our government sometimes lies to us about important events. . . . Over the 1960s, I became so skeptical about government pronouncements that I suspected that the television images of the first moon landing were staged in some warehouse."[39]

He believed, like all rational choice theorists, that it was naïve to think that government operated on ideals. "The beginning of wisdom," he wrote in his influential *Bureaucracy and Representative Government*, "is the recognition that bureaucrats are people who are, at least, not entirely motivated by the general welfare or the interests of the state."

Niskanen interpreted the behavior of bureaucrats as a response to the incentives they faced. Society, through its political representatives, desires services from government: administration, policy implementation, the solving of crimes, the provision of security, and so on. These are services that the free market will not naturally provide. Society therefore creates a bureau—such as *Yes, Minister*'s Department of Administrative Affairs—to supply these services. Bureaus provide services not on a per unit basis (x number of dollars per crime solved), as would a commercial business, but in return for a block grant or appropriation. (This is because society, not knowing, for example, precisely how many crimes will be committed in the coming year, cannot specify exactly and in advance what services will be necessary and so creates a body with general responsibility for their provision.)

Niskanen's analysis led him to a worrying conclusion. He reasoned that a bureau would have more information about the cost of providing services than would society, as represented through its legislative and executive institutions. Bureaucrats have no profit incentive; they cannot keep for themselves the difference between their appropriation and the cost of providing the service. But they do have an incentive to seek the largest budget they can get. The head of a bureau will desire more staff, better facilities, and more prestige. Seeing the world through the prism of their bureaucracy, they may also come to believe that more of the services provided by their office is good for society as a whole. In short, bureaucrats are incentivized to seek a more magnificent empire by obtaining the maximum funding possible.

The political institutions representing society, Niskanen posited, reveal how much they are willing to pay for each unit of service the bureau provides. Only the bureau knows how much each unit really costs, so with their incentive to gain as many resources as possible, the bureau oversupplies its services to society. Considered a matter of the public good, society wants the most efficient provision of services on a bureau-by-bureau basis so that it can allocate its resources for maximum possible overall benefit. But each bureau considers only its own interests rather than those of society in general. It oversupplies its services and so overcharges society. *Yes, Minister*'s Sir Humphrey is the embodiment of the Niskanenean bureaucrat, padding his empire at the public expense.

Niskanen's work suggested that government was consistently too big and doing too much. In attempting to solve the undersupply of services in a pure market situation, modern democracies had created massively wasteful oversupply—a gospel that Niskanen preached with great fervor during the Reagan years and in which Margaret Thatcher, too, fully believed. The only solution, Niskanen, Thatcher, and Reagan believed, was to "starve the beast" of government and shift as many of its functions as possible to the private sector, where they would be exposed to market pressures.

The Niskanenean analysis swept the academic world, too, although scholars quickly began to refine some of its postulates. Working in the public choice tradition, political scientists Terry Moe and Gary Miller were impressed with Niskanen's approach but puzzled by one of his assumptions: why were bureaucrats posited to be so much better at strategy than politicians? Why, in a recurrent negotiation involving vital policy matters and vast sums of money, would politicians simply tell bureaucrats how much they were willing to pay for each level of service and then let the officials decide for themselves how much service to provide? This assumed a degree of naïveté on the part of the legislature that seemed inconsistent with the utility-maximizing assumptions of rational choice theory.[40]

Miller and Moe accepted Niskanen's supply-and-demand framework. They agreed that the bureau was a monopoly service supplier with all the potential for bloated costs that implies. However, they believed Niskanen had failed to adequately model the other side of the equation: the legislature. It, too, is a monopoly buyer. The bureau has no one else who is a potential purchaser of its services, so the legislature has the leverage to control costs.

And the incentive: it is filled with politicians seeking reelection from a public that does not like to see its tax money wasted. Instead of the passive and naïve politicians of Niskanenean analysis, Miller and Moe imagined legislators to be aggressive cross-examiners of bureaucrats. Under scrutiny from the only customer for their services, bureaucrats would have to be more transparent and cost-sensitive than Niskanen assumed.

Miller and Moe thought Niskanen had erred further in talking of the legislature as an undifferentiated whole rather than, as in reality, a body divided into specialized committees. It is the committees, composed of legislators who are expert in specific policy areas and knowing that whatever they agree must at some point be ratified by the body as a whole, that engage in budget negotiations with the bureau. Legislators in committee have the expertise to second-guess bloated bureaucratic estimates and are compelled to consider the general interest.

The problem as conceptualized by Miller and Moe, then, is not that the bureaucracy has an unassailable information advantage over the politicians. The problem is ensuring that legislators carry out the oversight functions for which they are equipped. Miller and Moe argued that Niskanen's solution—privatization of government services—would only make the problem worse. Unlike public bureaus, private companies have a strong profit incentive and will simply pocket any appropriation beyond what it costs to supply services. Moreover, as private firms, they may be able to shield themselves from oversight in a way that public bureaus cannot.

The twin analyses of Niskanen and Miller-Moe neatly mirrored the views of government encoded into *Yes, Minister* by Antony Jay and Jonathan Lynn. For Jay, a conservative, the problem of government was Niskanenean in nature: the bureaucracy was irredeemably wasteful and should be pared back and, as much as possible, placed in private hands. For Lynn, with his more pro-government bent, the issue was how to compel lazy elites to act in the public interest. The Miller-Moe analysis more closely reflected his views. Privatization would make the problem worse, as British left-wing thinking of the time argued.

This more balanced view of the interests and behavior of bureaucracies now dominates political science. It has been refined by a triptych of political scientists, Matthew McCubbins, Kenneth Noll, and Barry Weingast (collectively, and rather charmingly, referred to as McNollgast) into the "principal-agent" approach.[41] Just as a homeowner (the principal) hires a contractor (the agent) to remodel a kitchen, finding it more efficient than learning how to do the work themselves, so government (principal) hires a bureau (agent) to do a specialized job.

Principal and agent agree a contract—what work will be done on what schedule and at what cost—and then the principal has an array of means to ensure that the job is carried out. They can monitor the agent through observation, seek progress reports, and build incentives and penalties into the contract for meeting or missing deadlines. Both sides have private interests and both sides are active in pursuing them, but an engaged principal should be able to ensure broad compliance from their agent. In this way the government can tame the bureaucracy.[42]

This evolution in public choice thought about bureaucracy mirrors the evolution of the Hacker–Sir Humphrey relationship in *Yes, Minister* and *Yes, Prime Minister*. Hacker is at first as helpless as Niskanen's politicians, and Sir Humphrey largely succeeds in pursuing his private interest. But over time, as Hacker learns on the job, he becomes wise to Sir Humphrey's tricks and the relationship grows more equal. As prime minister, Hacker often has Sir Humphrey on the run, developing multiple sources of information about what is going on in government and flexing his muscles as the preeminent politician in the land.

Legacy

Yes, Minister started as a sit-com and became an icon. The British public was shown the hidden workings of government and the curtailed nature of British democracy, how hard the elite worked to deny them real political choice and to frustrate efforts at change. Government ministers in the 1980s and 1990s took to calling their permanent secretaries "Sir Humphrey," and, famously, the Department of Transport borrowed the plot device of a season 3 episode on an integrated transport policy as the inspiration for a set of real policy innovations.[43]

The satirist Armando Iannucci argued, in a BBC documentary, that *Yes, Minister* was the best British comedy series ever made. "It's a mark of the show's subversive influence," he said, "that we now cannot trust a politician if he sounds like a character from *Yes, Minister*, or deploys the sort of malformed logic for which the programme was famous. If it's depressing that this sort of logic is still used, it's a cause for rejoicing that we now have the means to identify it."[44]

The view of the political elite in *Yes, Minister* is unlovely. It is a testament to the skill of the actors and the writers that the show remains charming viewing. The meaning made of politics was that it was an elite game played by venal schemers. Worse, the public's elected representatives were bad at this game. Read through the political science of bureaucracy, this image is only reinforced. As Jonathan Lynn noted, the message *Yes, Minister* delivered to the non-elite was that far more effort was made to keep them out of government deliberations than to make sure policy served their interests.[45]

Politicians found *Yes, Minister* uncomfortably close to home. For many of the generation that came of age in the 1970s and 1980s, *Yes, Minister* was their formative political touchstone. They were determined to avoid becoming hapless captives of the civil service.

Hacker had eventually gotten the better of Sir Humphrey by developing his own sources of information and advice, independent of the bureaucracy. When he became prime minister, he gained a personal adviser. Thus, at the end of the series, Hacker reversed his fatal defenestration in episode 1, where he had allowed Sir Humphrey to separate him from his political adviser, who became a seldom-seen figure and eventually disappeared from the show entirely.

The *Yes, Minister* generation of politicians took note, and when they became senior figures, they acquired whole cadres of advisers who were loyal to them, not to the permanent machinery of government. Bernard Donoughue, an adviser to Harold Wilson and a key consultant to Jay and Lynn, later joined Tony Blair's Labour government and worked alongside this new generation. "These were young people who'd grown up watching the show," Donoughue said. "And some of them came in, as a consequence, excessively primed, and were out to demonstrate their masculinity by not listening to their civil servants. And I think they went too far. Because they were young, inexperienced ministers, and they hadn't a clue what to do. . . . But you could really hear them say this: 'I'm not going to let Sir Humphrey run me!'"[46]

In *Yes, Minister*, then, government is interpreted as a struggle between the private interests of the politicians and the bureaucrats, with the public good a seldom-noted consideration. The creators of the show encoded it with critiques circulating among the political left and the right, as well as with a remarkable degree of verisimilitude brought about by their extensive research and the whistle-blowing efforts of Richard Crossman and Leslie Shipman. When *Yes, Minister* was decoded by the audience, the public gained enormous insight into the behind-closed-doors workings of the British state. Among this audience were many future politicians, who internalized the lesson of *Yes, Minister* and took great pains to avoid becoming captives of the civil service.

For Armando Iannucci the temptation to update *Yes, Minister* for a new, more cynical political age, dominated by special advisers and yet still inhabited by feckless politicians, was too great to resist. It is to his political fictions—*The Thick of It* and its US translation, *Veep*, that we turn in the following chapter.

7 | Farce—*The Thick of It, Veep*

On September 11, 2001, Jo Moore, a British government official, sent an email to her colleagues: this was "a good day to bury bad news."[1] Moore was a special adviser in the Department of Transport, Local Government, and the Regions. She worked alongside the permanent civil servants but reported directly to Stephen Byers, the minister at the head of the department. Small numbers of special advisers had been a feature of British government since the mid-1960s. They were supposed to give senior politicians policy advice but play a secondary role to the career civil service. The Labour government of Tony Blair dramatically increased their number and enhanced their status; special advisers would now be aggressive bureaucratic warriors and partisan media operatives. They saw their role as spinning the news and promoting the impression of good government, whatever the underlying reality.

Jo Moore's email was received with horror. The civil servants in her department thought it was crass and inappropriate. The 9/11 email was not her first offense. Moore had asked civil servants to leak stories to the press. She ordered them around. Her civil service boss had tried to remove her, only to find that she was protected by Stephen Byers, the minister. For Byers she was a valued personal aide and a counterweight to the power of the permanent bureaucracy. As a concession to the civil servants, Byers sanctioned the hire of former BBC journalist Martin Sixsmith. He was brought into the department as the director of communications and tasked with keeping the peace.

An uneasy truce prevailed until February 2002, when Moore decided that the day of Princess Margaret's funeral—sure to be the first story on the news—would be a pretty good time to release some pretty bad statistics about the state of Britain's railways. Sixsmith learned of this and emailed the whole department, writing, "There is no way I will allow any substantive announcements next Friday. Princess Margaret is being buried on that day. I will absolutely not allow anything else to be."

There was now a full-blown war within the department. While Byers was close to Jo Moore, Sir Richard Mottram, the senior civil servant, found that his staff, led by Sixsmith, were unwilling to work with her. Byers and Mottram reached a compromise: Jo Moore would resign and so would Martin Sixsmith. The stories—about Princess Margaret's funeral, the 9/11 email, the leaked tales of department infighting—would be described as "unfortunate events" with no blame attached to anyone.

The resignations of Moore and Martin Sixsmith were duly announced, with only one problem: no one had told Sixsmith. He went straight to the press with his story of being "unilaterally resigned."[2] Sixsmith detected the hands of the prime minister's office, particularly his ultra-powerful director of communications and strategy, Alastair Campbell. Campbell, like Moore, was a special adviser, but working for the prime minister gave him vast power, which he exploited to the maximum.

Blair's government had acquired a reputation for the hyperactive spinning of stories and for damaging infighting between special advisers and the civil service. Their preoccupation with media appearances often backfired, causing more damage to the government than if they had simply shared whatever bad news they were trying to cover up. In this case the minister himself, Stephen Byers, was forced to resign over what was essentially office politics among his subordinates.

Sixsmith settled his dispute and left the civil service. He was expected to write an excoriating memoir about the experience but turned instead to fiction. He began to work with the satirist Armando Iannucci on an idea for a television show about spin, special advisers, and the new politics of the era. It was called *The Thick of It*.

The image reconstructed in this chapter is of politics as *farce*. A farcical situation is one where great energy is expended with counterproductive results. Politics in *The Thick of It* is interpreted as game playing and office infighting. The political elite are portrayed as having few fixed beliefs and being broadly incompetent yet desperate to maintain a public image of complete control over events. Politicians, spin doctors, and bureaucrats fight vicious internal battles to prevent the public from seeing how flaccid and vapid government really is. The elite are engaged in a never-ending war against one another over who should take the blame for the constant cock-ups. Skilled and resourceful at fighting behind closed doors, they are irresponsible, insincere, and inarticulate in public.

This chapter should be read, then, as closely linked to the last. Both deal with the problem of political control of the bureaucracy, of intra-elite infighting, and of the titanic energies expended to make sure the public never, ever sees what really happens in government. Special advisers, that defining cadre of modern British government, are the muscle politicians employ to wrest control from career bureaucrats. Yet reliance on special advisers has further distanced the political elite from the people they serve.

The Thick of It speaks also of so-called third way or neoliberal politics in the UK and the US, the kind of politics that perhaps was extinguished by Hillary Clinton's loss to Donald Trump in the 2016 presidential election. After devastating losses in the 1980s to Thatcher and Reagan, the Democrats under Bill Clinton and the Labour Party under Tony Blair had shed many of their ideological commitments and promised a centrist, technocratic form of government. These reformed center-left parties embraced the market-led prosperity of globalization while, in theory at least, smartly using government to mitigate economic inequality. Embracing the market meant abandoning leftist policy commitments, and adopting the guise of business-friendly competence meant enforcing rigid message discipline so that government appeared modern and well-run. The boundary between left and right now collapsed, to be replaced with a presentation-obsessed technocratic centrism.

These two moves—ditching ideology and presenting an external image of managerial competence—stripped politics of the final vestiges of authenticity and left it on the brink of Trump and Brexit. In the UK, Blair's techniques provoked suspicion that his government—and the imitative successor governments of Gordon Brown and David Cameron—was empty at its core, concerned with spin rather than policy. The so-called culture of spin became the major objection to the Blairite project, the efforts expended for appearances' sake seen as increasingly absurd and self-defeating.

The Thick of It captures an era in British politics—and US politics too—where presentation seemed to throttle substance.[3] Until the year of Brexit and Trump—the subjects of the next chapter—this was thought to be a permanent condition of a globalized, increasingly post-ideological world.[4]

The Thick of It

"The truth goes something like this," begins Armando Iannucci, introducing *The Thick of It*. "Ministers have very little power." Instead, power lies with "a gang of political bouncers" like Alastair Campbell, who careen around the ministries to make sure everyone is on message. Politics is driven by these behind-the-scenes fixers and by fear of the media, espe-

cially the tabloid press. Ministerial existence is an absurd exercise of cur-
rying favor with a thuggish center of government and a rapacious populist
press. Appearances dominate—indeed effectively constitute—reality.[5]

As *The Thick of It* opens, a nondescript middle-age man enters the fictional Ministry of Social Affairs. This man is the minister, Cliff, who bum-
bles his way upstairs to be confronted by Malcolm Tucker, the prime minister's special adviser. Cliff is terrified. Malcolm reassures him that he is
doing a good job. The prime minister has no desire to remove him from
his post. Cliff is relieved. He offers Malcolm some fruit.

But here's the thing, Malcolm continues. The string of negative head-
lines about the minister, about his department, is making things "difficult."
Like Martin Sixsmith, Cliff is about to be "resigned"—the act of being
fired and told to say you left of your own accord. His attempts to plead his
case are rejected by Tucker, who transitions from charming to snarling in
an instant. "You've had a good innings. You've been here for eighteen
months. I've written some very nice things about you in the PM's reply to
your resignation." The minister's fate is sealed, and *The Thick of It*, after just
three minutes of the Age of Cliff, repeats its cold open, this time with
"Hugh," a new minister.

Malcolm Tucker is the central figure in *The Thick of It*. He is a composite of the cadre of macho spin doctors who maintained discipline in the
image-obsessed Labour governments of Tony Blair and Gordon Brown.
These practices migrated to David Cameron's Conservative Party after it
returned to power, making special adviser culture a bipartisan feature of
British politics.[6]

Tucker's management style is a mix of personal abuse and political de-
capitation. "Malcolm Tucker isn't meant to be Alastair Campbell," demurs
Iannucci, "but more a personification of many, many different people who
lurk in Number 10 and go around ministries telling people what to do—or
who ring up journalists and shout at them for not writing what they want."
Indeed, while Campbell is the most direct inspiration, Tucker contains
multitudes: there are bits in there of other notorious spin doctors of the
period like Peter Mandelson, Charlie Whelan, and Damian McBride.

Tucker will summon a minister to be shouted at and, while the victim
hurries to his office, pick up the phone to some other part of government for
an "interim shouting."[7] He appears as if from nowhere, seeming to material-
ize one millimeter from his target's face. Hugh Abbot, the minister, is frequently startled by Tucker's accomplishing this feat in the open-plan Social
Affairs building: "Christ, Malcolm! How do you appear out of nowhere in a
building made entirely of glass?" Tucker: "I'm a shape-shifter."[8]

In dealing with a recalcitrant minister, he advocates a variation of an established negotiation technique: "We should use the carrot and stick approach: you take the carrot, stick it up his arse, followed by the stick, followed by an even bigger, rougher carrot."[9] At one point he proposes to replace a failing official by tearing out his appendix, throwing the official away, and appointing the useless flap of colon to the position.[10] This approach extends to solving minor office problems. Do you know how to clear a paper jam, Malcolm? "Kill a kid an hour until it sorts itself out?"[11]

In *The Thick of It*'s interpretation of politics, the elected representatives of the people are useless. Those in government can be easily replaced via manipulations by special advisers and other intra-elite plots and thus live terrified lives. When Hugh Abbot disappears without explanation, he is succeeded as minister by Nicola Murray, whom her coworkers describe as "a shit politician pretending to be a mediocre one."[12] Asking whether she understands policy, Tucker says, is like asking if a dog grasps the concept of Norway.[13] He describes her media appearances as "like a clown running across a minefield." Listening to her on the radio makes him want to "tear off my eyelids and scrunch them up into ear plugs." She is, in a word Tucker coined that entered the British political lexicon, an "omnishambles." "From bean to cup," he tells her, "you fuck up."[14]

The conduct of good government is a rarely vocalized concern. The politicians in the show have utter contempt for the public they serve. "Sometimes when you meet the actual people," Hugh Abbot reflects, "you just look at their little beady eyes and mean little smiles. . . . They're from a different fucking species."[15] Policy is an exercise in free association. Terri Coverley, a career civil servant, implores the nexus of politicians and special advisers to "stop making policy on the hoof. If there could just be some sitting down involved." But it doesn't matter anyway. There is no money in the Department of Social Affairs and essentially no implementation capacity even if they came up with a workable idea.[16]

The culture is execrably macho, with Tucker a genuine political killer and the other men being mostly terrified but fancying themselves as locker-room louts. "They stand around chattering like squirrels on Red Bull," says a female coworker, "and when you ask them what they are talking about they bark a tea order at you."[17]

The meta-joke is that the screaming, frantic activity is self-defeating. The end result, as in all farce, is made worse by the attempts of the protagonists to intervene. "Reading about the inner workings of the Blair government," Iannucci recalls, "what I always thought was very funny was the fact that they always made things worse by worrying too much."[18]

Special Adviser Culture and the Age of Alastair Campbell

The rationale for the appointment of special advisers (who came to be known as SpAds) is to bring expertise from other spheres of life into government. In principle this allows experts to give additional information to the minister, yet in practice most of their time is spent on appearances rather than substance.[19]

Most special advisers work in messaging and strategy; the most notorious are those attached to a prominent member of the government; the most prominent of all is attached to the prime minister. Drawn largely from the ranks of tabloid journalism and party activism, these SpAds challenged the traditional dominance of civil servants. They were avowedly partisan, whereas the civil service was required to be politically neutral. The line between partisan activities and merely discharging the government's business was often hard to maintain. SpAds didn't fit into the hierarchical management system either. Appointed to civil service jobs yet serving at the pleasure of their minister, they often proved to be beyond the control of anyone.

They were not socialized into the Whitehall culture of calm administration. They had sharper edges than the plummy Sir Humphrey's. Young and overwhelmingly male, they brought a crude sensibility into government. Where the senior civil servant would retire to the House of Commons tearoom to fix up a backroom deal, the special adviser was to be found in the pub telling tales over a lake of beer, or dashing around with a cell phone perma-glued to their ear. The senior civil servant might like to reference the classics to illustrate a point; the SpAd liked football and fancied himself as a bit of a hooligan.

They were aggressive in defense of their ministerial patrons and only semi-ethical in how they handled government communications. Far from mere vessels by which information was transmitted to the public, special advisers solicited favorable coverage by grooming particular journalists, giving them scoops, and freezing out or misleading their rivals. The SpAd got the story out while the journalist advanced their career with a stream of exclusives.

The most prominent special adviser of the era was the prime minister's director of communications and strategy, Alastair Campbell. When Campbell ran into Armando Iannucci at a political event in 2010, he called the writer/director "the bloke who's been making a living off me for the last ten years."[20] While Malcolm Tucker is an amalgam of several figures, indeed an embodiment of the entire culture of special adviser/media politics, Campbell is the central inspiration.

Alastair Campbell's origin story is tied up with that of Tony Blair. Campbell was a talented, if crude, left-leaning tabloid journalist in the 1980s when he spotted a new generation of media-savvy, centrist Labour Party figures who promised a path out of opposition for this tired old organization. Of these leaders—Gordon Brown, Peter Mandelson, and Tony Blair—Campbell saw instantly that it was Blair, with his upper-class background yet facility with populist rhetoric and ideological flexibility, who had the greatest potential. While the assumption of the cadre who formed New Labour was that Gordon Brown would be the leading figure, Campbell thought Blair was the man.

Of the adviser who would become his consigliere, some even thought his political brain, Blair had this to say:

> In my experience there are two types of crazy people: those who are just crazy, and who are therefore dangerous; and those whose craziness lends them creativity, strength, ingenuity, and verve. Alastair was of the latter sort. The problem with them is that they can be mercurial, difficult and on occasions even erupt with damaging consequences.[21]

Campbell could be astonishingly abusive toward the journalists he briefed every day. Peter Oborne, political correspondent for the *Daily Mail*, suffered for years his "routine barbarism." Campbell would walk into a room to brief journalists with a cheery "OK, you bastards. Explain to me just why I should waste my time with a load of fucking wankers like you when you're not going to write anything I tell you anyway."[22] On another occasion, BBC journalist Jeremy Vine dared to suggest he would cover Tony Blair's 1997 election campaign in the way he chose, according to his professional judgment. Campbell "went absolutely mad," Vine recalls, and said, "You will fucking report exactly what I tell you to report, you'll stick to my fucking schedule and nothing else."

Campbell's qualities were extreme devotion to the cause he was serving, an exquisite understanding of the dynamics of the British media, and ruthlessness veering into barbarism, yet leavened, when necessary, with a dash of charm.[23] As the prime minister's special adviser in charge of communications and strategy, his writ ran far and wide. Blair kept little from him and made it known that Campbell spoke with his voice. Ministers soon learned to fear him. "You go to Tony with a private problem," said one, "and he tells Alastair. Then later, if he wants to, he will use it [against you]."[24]

Campbell issued orders that ministers could not speak to the press without first gaining his permission. He coordinated policy announcements in a centralized "grid," with government actions spread out over the days of the week to make sure each received maximum attention or, if Campbell deemed it desirable, was buried under something else. Martin Sixsmith, the head of communications at the transport department who clashed with Jo Moore, recalls how Campbell dealt with personnel gathered from across government in meetings each morning:

> He would sweep in with a breezy "Morning, you lot!" and a Burnley FC mug of tea, before launching into a series of quick-fire demands on how the Cabinet should tackle the day ahead. It is Campbell who decides what the ministers will say, including the prime minister. "We'll get TB to do this and say that," is the way he puts it.[25]

Campbell thought his methods were necessary in a twenty-four-hour media age. The government must speak with one voice, and authority must be centralized, so that ministers can work toward a common purpose and convey that purpose to the public. If ministers are allowed to talk to the media whenever they want and launch policies on their own schedule, then coherence will be lost. "Communications was not something that you tagged on at the end, it is part of what you do," he would tell colleagues.[26]

In pursuit of that coherence no one, including the prime minister himself, was spared.[27] When the two men were together, it was hard to tell who was in charge. Campbell would talk down to Blair, interrupting or contradicting him in media interviews. More than once, Campbell briefed the press about something the prime minister was going to say and failed to tell Blair himself, leaving the prime minister forlornly looking to his spin doctor for guidance. On other occasions, he would simply order Blair about, extracting him from meetings with a brusque "Come on, Tony, we're off. Get a fucking move on."[28]

It was in dealing with crises, though, that Campbell was at his most brutal. Campbell felt that most ministers were fallen persons with complicated lives that could at any point erupt into public view. He knew that personal foibles could damage the government but could also be weaponized in internal struggles. He had an encyclopedic knowledge of the peccadillos of senior politicians, and he could be fabulously indiscreet about them.

When Blair formed his first government in 1997, Campbell took it upon himself to talk to senior civil servants about how cabinet meetings would be run. He looked over a seating chart for the first gathering. "Let me tell you about this lot," he said to the assembled civil servants. He ran through each minister's weakness one-by-one. "Mmmm, likes the women . . . has a colorful past. . . . [These two] hate each other's guts."

Finally he got to the new foreign secretary. "Robin Cook," Campbell considered. "He has interesting arrangements with his secretary."[29] Cook was involved in a long-term affair with Gaynor Regan, his assistant. Three months into the Blair government, Campbell was told by a tabloid journalist that his paper had the story and was about to break it. The full force of the Alastair Campbell crisis management approach was deployed.

With a mixture of threats and charm, Campbell prevailed upon the journalist to hold the story for a few hours in return for a statement from Cook on the affair. Then he called the foreign secretary, who was at the airport with his wife, waiting to go on vacation. What happened next became the stuff of legend. Campbell told Cook he had to choose between his wife and his mistress, and he must do so immediately. A spin doctor was giving an ultimatum to the British foreign secretary about the central decision of his private life.

Such was Campbell's power that Cook didn't hesitate. "I'm afraid there isn't going to be a holiday, Margaret," he told his wife in the departure lounge, before telling the press his marriage was over and he was starting a new life with Gaynor Regan.[30] This was the first instance of what would become a pattern with Campbell: the attempt to exert total control would rebound with spectacular effect. Margaret Cook was not inclined to go quietly into oblivion, and she launched a sustained public attack not only on the ethics of her husband but also on the absurd situation of her marriage having been ended at the diktat of the British government's chief spin doctor.[31]

The Downfall of Alastair Campbell

A certain glamour attended the work of the spin doctors in the early New Labour years. There was the importation of American practices from the much admired Bill Clinton campaign, combined with the macho, hard-drinking culture of the Westminster fixer, and the undeniable fact that slick communications were central to the rout of the Tories in the 1997 and 2001 general elections. To be a spin doctor meant to be at the center of politics, making things happen, jousting with the press. It was all fun and games until someone got hurt.

The critiques of Tony Blair have a curious bifurcation. In domestic politics he was regarded as insubstantial, lacking ideological conviction, a cynical seeker of public approval, and, by consequence, reliant upon spin doctors to burnish his image by manipulating the truth. In foreign affairs the critique is the opposite: he listened too little to the public and was driven by a messianic worldview upon which he would not compromise.

The War in Iraq was the crucible in which these two critiques collided. And Alastair Campbell was at the center of it. Blair was having trouble convincing the British public of the wisdom of going to war alongside George W. Bush. The prime minister argued that Saddam Hussein was a grave threat to national security and a serial abuser of human rights; many in the public thought that Blair was simply doing Bush's bidding.

Campbell took it upon himself to bolster Blair's case.[32] He would put together a public presentation of intelligence on Saddam's regime. He recruited a group of young officials from the foreign office to work on the project; "Alastair's boys" they were called. "We are going to win this bloody war," Campbell told them. "And the first thing we need to do is to win the information war—and you are the people who are going to do it."

Alastair's boys pulled together a dossier of intelligence on Saddam's weapons of mass destruction (WMD), released in September 2002. The raw intelligence was suggestive but lacked a smoking gun about Saddam's WMD misdeeds. Campbell, the former tabloid journalist, knew that what was most important was a dramatic headline. He pushed to make sure the dossier was vivid, even lurid, in detail. In true spin doctor fashion, he offered to help a few friendly journalists with their interpretation of the document.

"Brits 45 Minutes from Doom!" read the headline in *The Sun* newspaper the day the dossier was released. The headline was stronger than the detail could support, though. It was possible Saddam had some missiles that could be launched forty-five minutes after an order to do so, though they could only reach British armed forces deployed near Iraq, and it was not clear that the munitions they carried were especially doom-some.

The dossier did not have the desired effect, so Alastair's boys went back to work. A new dossier, published on the eve of war and focused on human rights abuses in Saddam's Iraq, was compiled. It was hair-raising stuff. There was little doubt that Saddam was a monster. But in their haste, Alastair's boys had been sloppy with their sources. Substantial portions of the dossier were lifted from a graduate student thesis by a scholar in California. Not only had Alastair's boys not given credit, but they had cut-and-pasted so directly as to incorporate the grammatical mistakes of the original.

The press was soon onto them, destroying any hope that the dossier would bolster the case for war. Worse, the plagiarism prompted questions about what else was awry in the case against Saddam. On the morning of May 29, 2003, as coalition forces were struggling to impose order in post-Saddam Iraq, BBC defense correspondent Andrew Gilligan went on air with an explosive story: the September "forty-five-minute" dossier had been, in Gilligan's memorable words, "sexed up" by Alastair Campbell, who had pushed for it to include claims that he "probably knew to be false."[33]

Campbell reacted with the indignation of a man who had stopped just short of doing the thing of which he was accused. His aggressive spinning of the case for war must now be spun further. Step one in the spin doctor's playbook is to find some weakness in the damaging story, a trivial detail if necessary, and use that to discredit the entire case. Gilligan had spoken on air of having an intelligence source for his story. Campbell launched a frantic search for this source.

He was careening out of control, becoming obsessive. He was called by the House of Commons Foreign Affairs Committee to testify on the "sexing up" charges. His performance was agitated. Seated before the committee members, he made "slashing gestures" with his hands as he defended himself against having "connived to persuade parliament to send British forces into action on a lie." The allegation was outrageous, Campbell continued. "And I tell you. Until the BBC acknowledges that it is a lie, I will keep banging on. . . . They had better issue an apology pretty quick."[34]

Two days later Campbell was at the Wimbledon tennis finals trying to take his mind off things. Unable to do so, he left center court at 6 p.m. and raced across London, storming into the Channel 4 television studios, where the 7 p.m. news was about to go live. Producers saw that a massive news story, in the shape of the highly agitated director of communications for the prime minister, had walked through the front door. They ushered him straight onto live television.[35]

Chopping his hands up and down, hair askew across his forehead, red in the face, Campbell lit into the BBC's journalistic ethics. The Gilligan story was part of a media vendetta targeting phantom "evil spin doctors in the dark." It was based on a single, uncorroborated source, Campbell insisted.

A few days later Campbell was back on the case, asking a Ministry of Defense press officer to attack the BBC over the story. "If you want to get into a row with the BBC, go ahead, but don't involve me," the harassed press officer said. "But it's vital, it's vital," Campbell responded. "Alastair, stop it," tried the press officer. Campbell replied, "I can't. I can't. They're all after me. Everyone's after me."[36]

By the end of the first week of July, Campbell had found out the name of Gilligan's source. He was Dr. David Kelly, a WMD expert who worked for the Ministry of Defense and not, as Gilligan had asserted, the intelligence services. Campbell sought to use this factual error to discredit the whole story. Incredibly, Blair himself chaired multiple meetings in which they discussed how to make Kelly's name known. So many hints were dropped to various newspapers that it was easy to guess Kelly's identity. The Ministry of Defense offered to confirm the name to any journalist who correctly guessed it and to allow unlimited attempts. Reporters could have worked alphabetically through a Westminster phone book and got there eventually.

In a forty-six-second phone call from his Ministry of Defense employers, Dr. David Kelly was informed that he would be named as the source in the morning newspapers. He had been wracked with guilt over the whole affair. He had said more than he had intended to a friendly journalist. What he said was accurate, but he regretted talking to the media. He was also deeply offended that his credibility as an expert was being assailed in an attempt to discredit Andrew Gilligan's story and that his employers were so willing to throw him to the wolves.[37]

A little over a week later, amid relentless scrutiny of his actions and career, David Kelly told his wife that he was going for a walk in the woods, leaving their home in Oxfordshire at 3 p.m. in the afternoon. He sat down underneath a tree, took a large number of painkillers, and slit his left wrist.

Tony Blair was on a trip to the United States to receive the Congressional Medal of Freedom when he was told the news. A journalist asked him if he had blood on his hands. He turned white, looking like he was about to throw up. Alastair Campbell resigned shortly thereafter.

Veep

The Thick of It is imbued with the hardest of edges: not just the profanity and the macho, bullying culture, but the deep cynicism about politics as a game played by self-obsessed elites, with little thought for policy and the lives that it impacts. What Tony Blair had learned in opposition—about the importance of presentation and the supposed political toxicity of ideo-logical commitments—caused him endless problems when he over-applied these lessons in government.

His special advisers had been brought in to give him control, embraced by a generation of politicians that had internalized the danger of bureau-cratic capture they had seen on *Yes, Minister*. But when Margaret Thatcher had railed against the bureaucracy, she had a radical agenda to implement. Blair, and indeed Clinton, came into office as technocratic centrists. Their promise was that sensible government, friendly to the market, would reap the fruits of globalization for all sectors of their societies. Politics in this in-terregnum, which we might date from the end of the cold war to the onset of the global financial crisis, was imagined by the elite to be a post-ideological honeymoon from history. The role of government was to get out of the way of the market. That, at least, was the vision Blair and Clinton promoted, where anyone not on board with the inevitability of globalized markets and institutions was portrayed as backward-looking and dangerously extreme.

This is the substrate on which *The Thick of It* rests. It satirizes an era of politics where presentation replaced policy. The comedy lay in doing too much in pursuit of the image of competence, turning government into an exercise in absurdist farce. When Armando Iannucci was asked to bring the show to American TV, it soon became clear that *The Thick of It* would not translate directly. A couple of episodes, with the swearing bleeped out, were shown on BBC America. Given the proliferation of the profanity, the airing became essentially one long bleep. The pilot of a remake was at-tempted by a major American network, but it was disastrous.

Instead, for the US market Iannucci shifted the focus away from spin doctors and onto the inherently ridiculous position of the vice presidency, a heartbeat away from absolute power yet, while the president's heart keeps ticking, little more than a redundancy in the American political sys-tem. The farce in this show—called *Veep*—was provided by Vice President Selena Meyer, always one grasping reach short of acquiring real power though having no idea what she would do with it should she get it.

The setting was different, but the interpretation of politics is consistent from *The Thick of It* to *Veep*. The politicians are self-obsessed and indiffer-ent to the public, whom they distrust and attempt to deceive. Their efforts to do so are farcical. The political elite in *Veep* are hyper-verbal, skilled at generating cutting insults behind closed doors. This eloquence disappears in public, where they are reduced to stumbling and insincere platitudes. Their private eloquence is never deployed in service of sincere advocacy for political values. It is an imagination of politics as post-ideological, as vapidly free of ideals, as *The Thick of It*.

Veep provoked one glorious moment of premise-validating behavior from Hillary Clinton. Julia Louis-Dreyfus, who plays Vice President Meyer, was delighted to receive a note from Clinton, then secretary of state: "Dear Julia, Hope you get everything you want as Veep—gun control, immigration and education reform." Two years later, as part of the hacked Clinton emails, a second note from the same time period surfaced online. "A friend wants me to sign something for Julia Lewis-Dreyfus [sic] for Veep," Clinton wrote to an aide. "Any ideas?" Her aide replied, "Let me brainstorm on this one/do some research. I confess I haven't seen the show!" Dreyfus framed both notes and displays them side by side on her office wall.[38]

Hillary Clinton, the 2016 Democratic presidential candidate, was readily interpretable by theories and fictions about rationally acting elites, strategically maneuvering to occupy a focus-grouped policy space, to present a public image of manicured competence, to fight the intra-elite battles with her guile and Washington experience. A character based on Clinton could be cast in any of the political fictions we have analyzed so far. I show in the next chapter that Donald Trump, and the leaders of Brexit, could not. They are unintelligible through the scientific-rational construction of politics and via the grammar of popular interpretations of politics circulated by our televised fictions. A different vocabulary is needed to make meaning of them.

The Thick of It drew to a close in 2012 with a story arc about the practice of leaking information to journalists. Called to testify before a legal inquiry into this practice, Malcolm Tucker has to wrestle with the changes in the politics-media nexus that have taken place over the seven-year life of this political fiction. By 2012 the notion of a spin doctor seeking to shape a story by bullying mainstream media journalists seemed almost quaint, given the rise in social media and the fracturing of narrative that had resulted. Tucker has to confront his own obsolescence: he is "a political dinosaur." If he is to be made extinct, though, he will not go quietly. His closing monologue serves as an epitaph for this show and for the political culture it had captured with such concussive effect.

"The whole planet is leaking. Everyone is spewing up their guts onto the internet. We've come to the point where the exchange of private information is what drives our economy. You don't like it? Then you don't like yourselves. You don't like your species. Well, you know what? Neither do I."[39]

8 | Populism—*Black Mirror, The Apprentice*

Two era-defining events took place within a few months of each other in 2016. In March the people of the United Kingdom voted to leave the European Union in a move called Brexit. In November the people of the United States elected businessman and reality TV star Donald J. Trump as president. Both events came against the pleas of the governing elites. They shocked experts in opinion polling and political science. They signified the resurgence of populism in advanced Western democracies and the retreat of seemingly entrenched principles of transnational liberalism.[1]

Populism, a style of politics more than a precise ideology, champions the desires of the people against elites and outsiders.[2] The people are an imagined construct, signified by some combination of material status, education level, and ethnicity. Populists and their followers believe themselves to constitute a majority, whether as a matter of fact they do or do not. Populisms of the right, such as Trump and the Brexiteers, see themselves as guardians of the threatened traditions of the nation. Expertise is regarded with suspicion by populists, who elevate folk wisdom and the general will—all of these being, of course, subjectively defined categories.

The scientific and televisual fictions pulled together so far in this book make sense of politics as a game played by elites, fighting viciously behind closed doors while portraying a public image of platitudinous moderation. In some fictions, such as *The West Wing*, elites speak about the interests of the people, although they rarely engage with voters directly. *The West Wing* portrays politics as the province of extraordinary people from Ivy League universities. Most other fictions in this study—*House of Cards*; *Scandal*; *Yes, Minister*, the satires of Armando Iannucci—show elites engaged in internecine warfare that is either orthogonal or actively hostile to the interests of the people.

Political elites, as constructed in our televised fictions, have been repeatedly portrayed as disingenuous. They perform democratic pluralism in public, claiming to be good-faith integrators of the diverse interests of the societies they led. Yet in private they are consumed with internal battles and advancement of their narrow self-interest. Political science has hardly offered a more attractive view of elites. Portrayed as rational actors and studied as abstractions, they are interpreted as calculating and cynical. As political scientist Terry Moe told us, "Stop thinking of presidents [and all politicians] as people. Think of them generically, as faceless, nameless, institutional actors."

A compelling way to think about the shocks of 2016 is that voting publics grew tired of being deceived by interchangeable members of the political elite. When populist leaders came along, sufficient numbers of voters accepted the offer of a different style of politics, disregarding the warnings of a discredited elite.

Armando Iannucci, creator of *The Thick of It* and *Veep*, believed that the politicians he had satirized brought this upon themselves. Instead of acting authentically on the basis of ideals, the political class had focused ever more intently—and cynically—on smaller and smaller groups of swing voters.

[A] "tiny swing minority . . . just assuming everyone else would vote the way they'd always voted."

"Gradually, the mood has changed. The electorate has woken up to that and said, 'No, you can't take us for granted. We're going to vote differently.'

"And what has happened is it's all gone crazy."[3]

In this reading, the Brexiteers and Trump stomped on the desiccated framework of meaning surrounding our politics. Both movements took aim at elite constructs, be they international institutions, or mainstream policies, or norms of behavior, and found them to be hollow and disconnected from the needs and desires of voters. A politics of identity rather than rationality, of crude authenticity rather than airbrushed perfection, carried the day.

Brexit and Trump are rendered understandable, and in some sense were anticipated, by two televised fictions. *Black Mirror* is a dystopia, focused on the interaction between human nature and the technologies of the social media age. Its portrayal of the technologies of cyber-discourse provides significant interpretive resources for grasping the populist resurgence. *The Apprentice*, an American reality television show staring Donald Trump, is perhaps the key political text of the age. It transformed Trump from property mogul to national celebrity. Its discourse of success—as an achievement that comes from inherent ability and bold action rather than education and preparation—was an important validator of Trump's political style. This discourse is contra to that established by the political fictions we have examined so far. Their code of success is intellectual and cultural elitism. Far more people watched *The Apprentice* than these political fictions. Many of them internalized the image of Donald Trump as a more relatable leadership figure than, say, Jed Bartlet.

These fictions—*Black Mirror* and *The Apprentice*—are set in the context of the Brexit and Trump victories. The question stalking this chapter is therefore profound: have the new political meanings that cohered in these moments permanently shifted our vocabulary—and hence our very concepts—of politics?

The Waldo Moment

Before the EU referendum had been called and Donald Trump had started running for president, *Black Mirror* introduced Waldo, a screen avatar on a fictional British news-satire show.[4] He is an animated blue teddy bear with a set of crude catchphrases. All shtick and cynicism, his role is to puncture the pomposity of those politicians who unwisely agree to be interviewed by him.

Liam Monroe, a supercilious minister of the Conservative government, is his guest. "What is a po-li-ti-cian?" Waldo asks, drawing out each syllable. Monroe replies, "Someone who tries to make the world a fairer place." Standard guff from the political elite. Just reasonable enough to say with a straight face though likely to make the audience at home snort in derision. "Like Batman?" Waldo asks with faux innocence. "Do you beat people up?" The interview is excruciating, and the politician complains about it afterward, bemoaning declining standards of public discourse. So Waldo, or rather the failed comedian who operates his controls and provides his voice, decides that this blue virtual gremlin should oppose the minister in the coming election. "Vote Waldo."

In the campaign debates, Waldo refuses to engage on policy, seeking instead to derail the process. At one point, he claims to find the minister attractive and proves this by brandishing his erect cartoon penis. The minister, not unreasonably, dismisses him as a joke. "You're a joke," Waldo fires back: "You look less human than me, and I'm a made-up bear with a turquoise cock. Who are you? You're just an old attitude with new hair. No one takes you seriously. That's why no one votes. No one trusts your lot, because they know you don't give a shit about anything outside your bubble. Something's got to change."

Waldo surges in popularity. Establishment politics, the way professional politicians think and speak, is so toxic that he becomes "a mascot for the protest vote." He offers no alternate policies and aims only to disrupt. Yet he draws huge crowds wherever he goes. The media find him irresistible. "You're going to get your biggest ratings for months because I'm here," he tells one news anchor.

His rallies start to turn violent, largely at the instigation of Waldo himself. He offers five hundred dollars to the first person in the crowd to hit a dissenter, and the man is hospitalized. On election night, Liam Monroe narrowly beats Waldo into second place. Instead of conceding, Waldo offers another five hundred dollars to the first person to hit Monroe with a shoe. Footwear flies, and the screen fades to black.

Cut to a dark underpass. Jamie, the failed comedian who voiced Waldo, is destitute and sleeping rough. Masked paramilitary police sweep him out from the underpass and move him on, into a deserted city center filled with neon screens. It is some years in the future, and Waldo has gone global. The screens show Waldo's face on the tail fin of fighter jets, streaking away on bombing runs in the Middle East. He is in classrooms, drilling young children on social conformity. He is speaking Mandarin, and Spanish, and English, and in each case he is the face of a violent authoritarian nightmare.

Cut to March 2016. Donald Trump is on the precipice of securing the Republican presidential nomination. The Sunday morning political television shows all start with Trump interviews. On weekdays he is omnipresent on CNN and MSNBC, cable networks that have turned their schedules over to coverage of the political horse race. He calls in to one after another and is put on air to hold forth on the story of the day. "Trump is not just an instant ratings/circulation/clicks gold mine; he's the motherlode," says Ann Curry, the former *Today* anchor. "The truth is, the media has needed Trump like a crack addict needs a hit."[5]

"I'm going to build a wall," he explains over the telephone during one of these appearances, "and there'll be a big beautiful door in the wall for people to come through."[6] This is Trump's immigration policy; the wall is to be along the US border with Mexico. Like most of his policy statements, it is a combination of boastfulness, myth, and fantasy. Listening to Trump, veteran TV journalist Cokie Roberts alternates between audible laughter and exaggerated eye-rolls. Yet not everyone found Trump funny. Vicente

Fox, the president of Mexico, did not appreciate Trump's insistence that his country would foot the bill for the new border barrier. "I'm not paying for that fucking wall," he said.[7]

Even less funny was the simmering violence that began to appear at Trump rallies, like the one I attended in Fairfield, Connecticut. Protesters had begun to infiltrate the pro-Trump crowds, and his supporters reacted with jeers and, sometimes, flailing fists. At these rallies the candidate himself spoke the language of the street. "I love the old days," he said as one protester was escorted out by security. "Guys like that would be carried out on a stretcher." On another occasion, he bade farewell to an ejected protester by telling the crowd "I'd like to punch him in the face," exhorting them to "beat the crap out of him—I'll pay your legal fees!"[8] At the rally I attended, two college-age women suddenly held handmade protest signs aloft. These were quickly wrestled from their hands and torn up by the crowd while private security guards pushed their way through the packed hall and bundled the women away.

I had gone to the Connecticut rally with a couple of professor friends of mine. At one point Trump said that we wouldn't see Hillary Clinton visiting the state, as she was too lazy to make the trip. My friends and I smirked at each other. Ironic eyebrow raises were exchanged. We clever academics knew that smart political candidates spend their time only in battleground states. Rigorous political science research said so! A rally in the reliably blue state of Connecticut was a waste of Hillary's time—and Trump's. On election night, though, Trump won Michigan and Wisconsin, "reliably blue" states in the Midwest in which he had held rally after rally. States that she had hardly visited at all. It was enough to give him the presidency. So who was the real political expert?

In the center of the hall where Trump spoke was a platform for television cameras and tweeting journalists. The candidate was drawn to them like a moth to a flame. When a scuffle broke out and the cameras turned to cover it, he denounced the unfairness of the media. "They only cover it because they think protests are bad for Trump," he said. Later he launched into a denunciation of CNN, a network he said was "failing" and was supporting Hillary Clinton. He claimed to know which of the cameras was from CNN and that the light on the camera went dark every time he said something negative about the media. The crowd booed and stared at the cameras, trying to figure out which was from CNN. I couldn't tell. But there were no lights flickering on and off in response to Trump's comments. His ratings were too high for that. The cable networks carried his appearances live and in full. It all seemed so far removed from the normal

tenor of primary politics—besuited career politicians pedaling bro-
mides—as to constitute almost an alternate universe, one you were not
sure was entirely real.[9]

Brexit

While the US presidential campaign was taking shape, the United Kingdom voted to leave the European Union. To the transnational political
elite, the EU was a shining example of post-ideological politics. The sub-
duer of nationalist barbarism, maintained by an unelected technocracy, in
the minds of the elite it had brought peace and prosperity to a conflict-
ridden continent. In the UK the vast majority of the political elite, and the
consensus of the banking, industry, and other professional classes, were in
favor of remaining in the union. But a faction of the political class, concentrated in the Conservative Party, had never reconciled themselves to
close partnership with their continental neighbors.

Their standard-bearer had been Margaret Thatcher. She thought the
European Union was run by an effete and officious class of mandarins, so
many Sir Humphreys imposing unnecessary regulations, interfering in
the free play of markets. With her Manichean mind-set, she saw any gain
in power for the EU as a loss of sovereignty for the UK.[10]

Seeking to unify the Conservative Party and stave off the threat from
the anti-EU United Kingdom Independence Party, Prime Minister David
Cameron had called a referendum on continued British membership. He
thought he could comfortably secure a vote for remaining in the union.
Most of the public in Britain had only the vaguest of ideas about the European Union, what it did and how it worked. Turnout for elections to the
European Parliament was consistently low.

Cameron sought to place economics at the center of the argument.[11]
The prime minister argued that Britain would suffer from leaving the EU,
with its tightly integrated financial, services, and trade markets. The plan
was for the elite of politicians, bankers, and industry titans to explain this
to the people, scaring them a little if necessary. Leaving the EU would be a
leap into the dark. George Osborne, the chancellor of the exchequer, deployed what became known as "Project Fear." He predicted that a vote to
leave would lead to immediate tax hikes in an emergency budget.

Mark Carney, the independent governor of the Bank of England, said
that leaving the EU would cause a recession. Even President Barack
Obama, visiting the UK at the height of the campaign, issued a stiff warn-

ing about the risks of leaving. The US had a relationship with the European Union, not Britain, Obama said. There would be no preferential trade deal post-Brexit, he said. The UK would "be at the back of the queue." This was classic elite vote-winning strategy, assuming that the inexpert public scared easily.

Yet the elite found that the economic warnings they issued, usually so effective in steering the electorate away from anything risky, were not working. As Kenneth Clarke, a pro-EU conservative party veteran, put it, "You can't actually have a referendum on the European Union, because no one really knows what it is." The "Leave" campaign had figured this out and refocused the debate. "If you start talking about immigration, then you can make some progress," Clarke noted.[12]

And so conservative politician Boris Johnson, the unconventional and charismatic leader of the Leave campaign, and Nigel Farage, zany founding father of the UK Independence Party (UKIP), promised to gain control of Britain's borders. The free markets of the European Union relied upon free movement of peoples among its members. While the elite focused on the economic benefits of free markets, the populist Leave campaign tapped into deep public resentment of immigration.

The cosmopolitan elite saw themselves as "citizens of the world." They understood, and benefited from, the free movement of labor. But some people believed that free movement meant foreigners taking their jobs or undercutting their wages. It meant strange-sounding people moving into their neighborhoods and stealing benefits. Whether the data supported their fears or whether they lived in close personal proximity to a significant number of immigrants didn't seem to matter: the idea took hold.

The populists Johnson and Farage played to this sentiment. Johnson, a sort of clown version of Winston Churchill, unkempt blond hair flying every which way, boarded a bus and toured the country to give stump speeches on the necessity of a Leave vote. Emblazoned along the side of his bus was a slogan: "We send the EU 350 million [GBP] per week. Let's fund our NHS [National Health Service] instead." It wasn't true, but it persuaded some voters.

Farage, meanwhile, pushed the issue of immigration: "Breaking point," screamed a UKIP poster, the slogan atop a photo of an endless stream of [by implication] Syrian refugees winding toward the British border. Again the claim was misleading: the photograph was of migrants crossing the Croatia-Slovenia border in 2015.[13] But it resonated. While experts rebutted the claims of Leave about the money going to the EU, and about the economic dangers of an exit vote, the Leave campaign barely engaged with the facts. Michael Gove, a prominent Leave campaigner, simply said, "People in this country have had enough of experts." And Farage's breaking point message, however disingenuous, was effective. "Immigration was snuffing out our ability to talk about the economy," said Will Straw, executive director of the Remain campaign.[14] The great irony was that the Remain campaign, still speaking the language of traditional politics, had encouraged Leave to focus on immigration. They thought that the issue would pale when set in the context of the wider economic arguments and that Leave politicians would come across as premodern extremists if they tried to demagogue it.[15]

By a margin of 52–48 percent, Britain voted to leave the EU, propelled, as an autopsy of the referendum campaign concluded, by "anti-establishment nihilism and anti-immigration siren-wailing."[16] The vocabulary of the elite consensus, perfectly encapsulated in the post-national, technocratic European Union, had failed to connect with voters.

Trump

Across the Atlantic, Hillary Clinton started to worry. Her branding in the 2016 presidential election was going to be essentially the same as the Remain campaign in Britain: I am the representative of a technocratic consensus that delivers economic prosperity and liberal values, the only sane approach to global order in an interconnected world. Would her message similarly fail to resonate?

Donald Trump, who took to calling himself "Mr. Brexit," saw only opportunity. He thought that the GOP establishment was weaker than it appeared. As journalist Matt Taibbi put it, an old and established party, with deep ideological convictions and a tight relationship between its leaders, activists, and voters, should be impossible to conquer by an outsider like Trump. The Republican Party establishment was instead revealed to be a small band of lawyers, mega-rich donors, and media intellectuals. Their candidate was Jeb Bush, upon whom they lavished $100 million. After Trump tagged him as "low energy,"[17] Bush won just 4 delegates of the 2,472 available.

Trump reimagined the GOP primaries as a reality TV show. He saw his competitors as boring characters unskilled in the art of grabbing attention. As they proved unable to define themselves, Trump did it for them, tagging them with unflattering nicknames and turning the debates into a series of political assassinations. In addition to Low Energy Jeb, there was Lyin' Ted Cruz, "Bible held high." There was Carly Fiorina, the only woman on the GOP stage, who Trump declared was too ugly to be president. And Little Marco Rubio, sweating uncontrollably.

GOP voters had become cognizant of the gap between the interests of the elite and their own, very different, views on trade and immigration. Establishment candidates like John McCain and Mitt Romney, foisted on primary voters by party elites in 2008 and 2012, had failed to win the presidency.

Did political science doom the Republican establishment?

The Party Decides was high profile, at least for an academic book.[18] Its thesis was that parties, not candidates, control the presidential nomination contest. This challenged the conventional wisdom that the rise of primary contests and the declining significance of party conventions had led to candidate-driven primary elections.

The book's authors, Marty Cohen, David Karol, Hans Noll, and John Zaller, believed that this dramatically understated the degree to which insiders shaped the process. The party elites did not trust the primary voters to pick the presidential candidate. They had two concerns. First, the early primary contests featured many candidates. Sometimes just 20 percent of the vote was all that was required to win the early primaries. Therefore, a candidate with a narrow yet intense appeal could win in the primaries but then be unable to prevail in the general election. Second, party elites thought that voters were swayed by charisma and glamour rather than policy and competence. A demagogue, ideologically out of line with the party elites, could win in the primaries.

Party insiders knew this, Cohen and his associates argued, yet had lost direct control of the nominating process since the reforms of the 1960s. The authors hypothesized that party insiders retained indirect control by colluding in preselecting a candidate before the first votes were cast. This "invisible primary" was the crucial contest, not the later, visible votes. During it, candidates had to signal that they held policy positions attractive to party insiders and that they could appeal to both primary and general election voters. Party insiders would help such a candidate win the nomination.

The party's most effective tool, the authors argued, was endorsements. Significant political figures—elected officials, donors, influential leaders of party-affiliated interest groups—would publicly support a candidate, giving them resources and, more important, identifying them as the pre-ferred insider choice. Early endorsements acted as signals among the party elite that a candidate had been chosen and could be parlayed into success with primary voters and in fund-raising. This continued until a single candidate grew so strong that they dominated the later primary contests, accruing enough votes to make the results of the visible prima-ries match those of the invisible primary.

The Party Decides was a remarkable work of imagination. By defini-tion, the invisible primary was unobservable. Positing its existence was therefore an act of interpretation, taking the apparently incoherent activi-ties of party elites and voters and trying to tell a story that made sense of them. The authors are quite clear that theirs is a creative work with real-world implications rather than an act of inductive observation.[19]

They conceptualized the invisible primary through game theory, spe-cifically a variant called the "restaurant game." Starting the evening in their respective apartments, three diners have to independently decide between three restaurants with three different menus. They receive a group discount if they all turn up at the same place. None of them can unilaterally chose a restaurant for the group, but they do know what type of food each restaurant serves, and what type of food each member of the group prefers. As each diner makes their choice, the rest of the group is notified.

Early restaurant choices function as signals to later deciders. If there is early convergence around a choice, then later diners either assume early deciders know the restaurant is good or, desiring the group discount, they follow the early movers anyway. A collectively rational choice emerges whereby not everyone gets their preferred type of food, but the menu is acceptable to most and all benefit from the group discount. In the analogy to nominations, the chosen candidate may not be everyone's first choice but should be broadly acceptable, and all benefit when they win the gen-eral election.[20]

The media help the party elites in the invisible primary, according to the theory. The horse race of the primaries makes for vivid stories. Jour-nalists determine, through backroom conversation with the party elite, who is the establishment favorite or the outsider and report this on air. They become one way of signaling the insider choice in the invisible pri-mary. The invisible primary is made visible, or at least audible, by the end-less circular conversation between politicians and journalists about which candidates and ideas are acceptable and hence likely to win. The reasoning quickly becomes circular: political journalists punish any candidate who steps outside the orthodoxy with a barrage of negative coverage, likely making them drop out of the race.[21]

It didn't work with Trump. Party insiders found him unacceptable on policy grounds and believed he would be a catastrophic general election candidate. Yet they could not stop him. The candidate who had won the invisible primary, Jeb Bush, had almost no appeal to actual primary voters. He was mauled in the debates by Trump. Other plausible insider candidates, such as Marco Rubio, fared little better.

With no consensus choice emerging from the early contests, the large Republican field divided the establishment vote among itself, allowing the outsider Trump to win most of the primaries. To have a chance at wresting back control of the nomination, the party elite needed to coalesce around a single opponent to Trump. That they would do so was the central thesis of *The Party Decides*. But it never happened.

Was *The Party Decides* a self-refuting prophecy?[22] Its thesis, that an insider candidate could be imagined into the nomination, was well known to party insiders and political journalists. In the 2012 campaign, evidence for it had seemed good on the Republican side. Outsiders such as Newt Gingrich and Rick Santorum rose briefly to the top of the polls and won a couple of contests, yet Mitt Romney, the consummate insider, outlasted them all, picking up establishment support until he had crushed all of his challengers.

The assumption in 2016 was that the same thing would happen to Trump. He would shine briefly then fade. His passionate supporters would then flock to another candidate. Waiting for this to happen, insider candidates did not drop out even when they had little support from primary voters. They were so sure that the invisible primary process would defeat Trump that they were already looking past it, attacking each other rather than Trump. Taking on Trump seemed risky: not only was he a talented counterpuncher, but they all wanted to vacuum up his voters after he dropped out, so they couldn't say anything too devastating about him.

This exposed a central paradox in *The Party Decides*, one that recurs in rational choice accounts of politics. The assumption of rationality in micro-level behavior allows for a focus on macro-level incentives and outcomes. But what if the micro-level actors simply assume the macro-level process will happen automatically and fail to take the actions necessary to make it happen? As Marty Cohen put it, "We think that it's in the party's interest to decide, and that they should be deciding." And yet the party did not.[23]

Thus the mistake of *The Party Decides* was to assume that the invisible primary was an automatic response to a recurring set of circumstances and part of a process amenable to scientific study. It was instead a set of hollow elite norms, tenuously tied together and relying upon the anticipatory compliance of the players—in particular the party insiders and the voters—for their effect on behavior. Put in the terms of this book, the invisible primary was a fiction, one that made sense in some but not all circumstances. Party elites—and political scientists—acted as if it were a universal and scientific fact.

Elite tactics, backed by seemingly solid political science research, had failed to prevent or predict the Brexit and Trump victories. Messages emphasizing the fear of economic instability, backed by strong elite signals to the public about which way to vote, had not delivered victory for David Cameron in the EU referendum. Imaginings about the invisible control of party elites over the nomination process, as well as conventional wisdom regarding the limits of acceptable policy positions and personal behavior, had failed to stop Trump.

The elite, as represented in expert theories of politics or in fictionalized portrayals on screen, had suffered stunning defeats at the hands of populist leaders. *Black Mirror*'s Waldo seems prescient, but it is the reality television show *The Apprentice* that is the key text in understanding what had happened.

The Apprentice

"This is a dictatorship, and I'm the dictator. There's no voting, there's no jury," says Donald Trump on *The Apprentice*, the hit reality television show that transformed his public image. The show had its origins in the convergence of interests of a TV network, a hotshot producer, and a billionaire tabloid playboy. First, the TV network NBC had come to realize that the new genre of reality television was a close to unbeatable financial proposition. Semi-scripted, and starring ordinary people rather than highly paid actors, production costs were low and ratings were high. Audience-grabbing conflict was guaranteed by casting combustible personalities, putting them in tense situations, and cleverly editing the results.

Second, *The Apprentice* was backed by the new king of reality TV, Mark Burnett. The young British TV producer had scored big with *Survivor*, his pioneering reality show about contestants marooned in exotic locales. NBC wanted more shows from him, and Burnett wanted to make something set in a major American city. He realized that the dynamics of survival in the Amazonian jungle were analogous to the dynamics of business in the concrete jungle of New York City.[24]

Third was the libertine tabloid star Donald J. Trump. The real estate developer had had an up-and-down career in business but possessed a genius for self-marketing. Burnett explained to Trump that he could use the show to rebrand himself. Trump was a staple of tabloid culture, portrayed as a reckless playboy with questionable business judgment. With a new television show, he could rehabilitate his public image.[25]

The Apprentice was born. The setup was that contestants, working in teams, took on a new sales and marketing assignment each week. Three members of the lowest-performing team would be called to a meeting with Trump in his boardroom, where one would be eliminated from the competition. At the end of the season, the winner would be offered an executive position within the Trump organization.

Much of *The Apprentice* was made up of standard reality show dynamics among the contestants, all of whom fit the usual criteria of being attractive and argumentative. The unique element was Trump himself. He played the role of the commanding decision maker, who set the contestants to work each week, monitored their progress by dropping in on them in his Trump-branded helicopter, and judged the results in the culminating boardroom scene at the end of each episode.

He is portrayed in the show as a reasoned and empirically driven boss. He asks for evidence before making decisions, relying on quantifiable measures such as profit margins and sales figures. He listens carefully to advice from "Carolyn and George," two senior managers from the Trump organization whom he assigns to work with the contestants. And although his harsh catchphrase in the show—"You're fired!"—was his own ad-libbed invention, he does not appear capricious or ad hominem in his decision making.[26] He expresses regret for having to let anyone go and wishes each contestant well as they are ejected from Trump Tower, a mythical palace of achievement, back onto the "killer streets" of New York City.[27]

Read through Trump's later political success, *The Apprentice* emerges as a key text. Its star, and his new vocabulary of politics, blew away the existing elite construction of politics as an insider game. The political implications of Trump's executive performance were clear. He was decisive, knowledgeable, tough, yet humane and paternalistic.[28] Some might even consider him progressive; he expressed a performance-based preference for the female contestants, at one point questioning whether he would ever hire a man again. The off-screen reality was apparently quite different. Rumors would later circulate about Trump's behavior toward female contestants and the racial attitudes he expressed. And the on-screen narrative of a coherent and wise executive was allegedly achieved by overdubbing of Trump's actual words and post-production editing to make his decisions seem evidence-based. Sometimes Trump would fire contestants for mysterious reasons, insiders recall. It was "our first priority on every episode like that," says Jonathon Braun, a supervising editor, "to make it look like his judgment had some basis in reality."[29]

The Apprentice was watched by far more people than the elite-driven political fictions we discussed in earlier chapters. Its first season, beginning in January 2004, averaged 27 million viewers. Thus Trump was a part of the mass popular consciousness for over a decade before his run for the presidency. As Trump was a populist candidate, so *The Apprentice* was populist television, the kind the elite avoids in favor of the hyper-verbal, intricately scripted political fictions that have been analyzed in this book.

Trump set a tone of meritocracy and focused on results rather than the identities of the contestants. The contestants on the first season of *The Apprentice* were diverse in terms of geography and level of education, in addition to race and gender. Much was made of Bowie, a "country boy" from Idaho with a high school education, who Trump liked.

Later, when *The Apprentice* became *The Celebrity Apprentice*, Trump was shown dominating the Hollywood elite. Linda Lucchese, a 2016 GOP convention delegate from Illinois who had never before been involved in politics, said she knew Trump from *The Celebrity Apprentice*: "All those celebrities. They showed him respect."[30] President Obama mocked Trump to his face about the fake nature of decisions in *The Apprentice*, but many Americans took the show seriously. Obama's mockery read to them as sneering elitism. *The Apprentice* is the kind of show Josh would have made a joke to Sam about on *The West Wing*. Jed Bartlet would never have heard of it.

The Apprentice legitimated a code of authority embodied by Trump. He is portrayed as a paternalistic executive, a person of inherent excellence whose success appears to have been achieved through bold action rather than preparation and education. Throughout the course of the show, he narrates an image of success that is focused on innate characteristics rather than learned mastery. "Negotiating is innate. It's in the genes. A negotiator is born."[31] His presentational skills are similarly natural: "I've never had lessons. I've always felt comfortable in front of a camera." The narrative is of internally driven talent that is not reliant upon expert input. "Either you're good at it or you're not."[32]

This suffused the attitude of the contestants as well. "Entrepreneurs shouldn't be spending much time in the classroom," says one.[33] Later in the season, they are given the task of selling art. Most candidly admit they have no art appraisal skills, so the interaction with buyers is a triumph of bullshit over expertise—the kind of expertise in art that non-elite Americans would not claim to have nor, perhaps, particularly value.

J. D. Vance, author of the best-selling memoir *Hillbilly Elegy*, became something of a celebrity in the 2016 political season. From desperate poverty in rural West Virginia, he later went to Yale Law School and became the cultural elite's translator of the "Trump voter." Vance explained that highly educated elite figures such as Barack and Michelle Obama were seen as threatening by some less-educated Americans.[34] They eloquently presented a narrative of success through education that seemed entirely out of reach. Yet the narrative of success in *The Apprentice*, based on succeeding through the beneficence of a tough yet empathetic patron, and reliance on chutzpah rather than expert credentialing, seemed much more attainable. Trump would not make them feel inferior and patronized as Barack and Michelle Obama and Hillary Clinton did.

In the first season finale of *The Apprentice*, Donald Trump chooses a contestant named Bill as the winner, and the walls of the boardroom open up to reveal a cheering studio audience. The boardroom is exposed as a fake, in the classic Potemkin-village style of reality TV. Trump then good-naturedly orchestrates waves of emotion from the crowd, offering a dream job to the winner, and cathartic encouragement to everyone else. Twelve years later he was elected president of the United States.

Fake News

In the opening episode of *Black Mirror*, the prime minister of the UK is sent a hostage video. Princess Susannah is being held by unknown forces and will be killed unless the prime minister has sex with a pig on live TV. It quickly becomes apparent that the British public like the princess a lot more than the prime minister and, by the way, would be quite amused to see him have sex with a pig. He has to go through with the act, which the public watch with rapt awe on screens in the pubs and the homes of the UK as the bedraggled princess, quietly released sometime earlier, stumbles unnoticed down the deserted streets of London. It is an acute commentary on the intersection of internet-era media culture, politics, and the darker impulses of the human mind: a combination of qualities that makes *Black Mirror* the second essential political text of the current era, taking its place alongside *The Apprentice*.

In September 2015, just before the ramp-up of the EU referendum campaign, Britain's *Daily Mail* newspaper ran an arresting headline: "British Prime Minister and Obscene Act with a Dead Pig's Head."[35] While studying at Oxford University, the article alleged, David Cameron had been part of an elite dining society, the initiation rites of which included the insertion of his penis into the mouth of said animal. Coming two years after the *Black Mirror* episode, reading this story was somewhat disconcerting for Charlie Brooker, the creator of the show. "That David Cameron was actually accused of doing something with a pig totally blew my brain. . . . I genuinely thought I lived in a simulation when that story broke."[36]

Black Mirror's central theme is the contested nature of reality and authenticity in an era of virtual immersion, where, as Brooker puts it, "you are constantly slipping into a little coma as you stare at one little screen after another."[37] The show's title refers to the dark, distorted image of oneself that comes from staring into a powered-down smartphone. The real darkness, though, comes after the phone is turned on.

By the year of Brexit and of Trump, internet sites such as Facebook and Twitter, originally seen as venues for social and political engagement, had gone sour. Both sites were flooded with "fake news"—manufactured stories containing outrageous falsehoods that were shared and re-shared among millions of users in what communication scholars call "information cascades."[38]

Fake news is manufactured on an industrial scale in surprising places. Beqa Latsabidse, a university student in Tbilisi, Georgia, set up a website posting stories about the 2016 American presidential election, hoping that high traffic volume would help him sell advertising on his site. Assuming that Hillary Clinton would win, he posted positive stories about her and waited for the hits to come. But no one cared, so he changed tack: he praised Trump and posted viciously anti-Hillary stories, many of which he copied from other websites, including from satirical sites.

In the hands of fake news sites like Latsabidse's, the satire was stripped away and a screaming headline affixed. The story was then reposted through Twitter and Facebook. Postings on these sites are given a uniform appearance, so it is hard to differentiate between a credible and incredible source. In early 2018 the special counsel Robert Mueller charged that, in addition to pop-up fake news sites like Latsabidse's, a coordinated campaign of electoral meddling by government-linked Russian entities had flooded US internet users with divisive and untrue social media stories.[39]

The information itself could be easily fact-checked. Taking it seriously required the willing suspension of disbelief.[40] These stories could gain traction only within a closed social environment inhabited by people who wanted to believe slanted stories—that is to say, in the exact environment created by the social media ecosystem. Facebook and Twitter rely on the self-selection of users into connected communities. At first these communities are persons known to the user directly, such as friends, coworkers, and family. But to expand beyond a few dozen "friends" or "followers" requires that the site provide suggestions, and these will be people who like similar things, click on similar sites and news stories, and thus offer the user little diversity of viewpoint. In addition, social media sites and web search tools like Google run algorithms to place in front of the user only content in which they are already interested, as deduced from their pattern of web use.

The scope of information and experience narrows and narrows until the algorithm has built a wall of mirrors around the user, reflecting their views and characteristics back to them. This is comfortable and efficient in that the user does not see things in which they are not interested. It is also dangerous in that their views go unchallenged and indeed seem to be universally shared by everyone around them.[41]

Commentator Katharine Viner saw this as the central dynamic of the Brexit and Trump victories. Viner recounts the shocked realization of Tom Steinberg, a web entrepreneur and supporter of remaining in the European Union, that he lived within an information bubble. The morning after the referendum, he went on the internet to try to understand what Leave supporters were thinking and feeling. "I am actively searching through Facebook for people celebrating the Brexit Leave victory," he wrote, "but the filter bubble is so strong and extends so far into things like Facebook's custom search that I can't find anyone who is happy despite the fact that over half the country is clearly jubilant today and despite the fact that I'm actively looking to hear what they are saying."[42]

These circumstances create epistemic communities of belief, and within these communities the most attention-grabbing members are rewarded. At the apex of one political epistemic community in 2016 was Donald J. Trump. He combined the tabloid sensibilities of the 1980s with a genius for the medium of Twitter, on which he had acquired a gigantic and loyal following. Many more people followed Trump than the subscriber base of, for example, the *New York Times*. While establishment politicians such as Barack Obama and Hillary Clinton used the medium cautiously, scared of a misplaced word or too hastily expressed view, Trump's tweets showed reckless abandon, and he proved himself a master of the form. "Trump will someday be in the Twitter Hall of Fame," journalist Matt Taibbi wrote. "His fortune-cookie mind—restless, confrontational, completely lacking in the shame/veracity filter—is perfectly engineered for the medium."[43] We might call this nexus between social media and fake news a populism of truth. Elite curators of fact, such as the media, have seen their expertise delegitimized and their influence dramatically reduced.

In September 2015, journalist Mark Leibovich took a campaign trip with Trump as he battled for the Republican Party nomination. Leibovich had had to convince himself to cover Trump, thinking him a joke and certain he would either drop out or be eliminated once the contest got serious. This had not happened. Trump was dominating the Republican field. Leibovich spent long days traveling with Trump, seeing him address pumped-up rallies and then marveling as the candidate, flying back home on his private jet, watched himself on cable news via a giant screen on the plane. Trump would give a little commentary on his performance. "Very presidential," he said approvingly, after one line landed particularly well.

Following a rally in Dallas, Leibovich flew on Trump's jet to Los Angeles. After eighteen hours of travel, a rally speech, and more travel, Leibovich was exhausted by the pace and the bombast, not comprehending how Trump, who sleeps only about four hours per night, was still going. As they were driven to Trump's Beverly Hills mansion, Leibovich finally saw him show fatigue. "Don't speak," Trump said as Leibovich got into the car with him. The journalist empathized with what he assumed was Trump's desire to switch off, to collect his thoughts and have a few minutes of privacy. This being the *Black Mirror* age, though, Leibovich could not resist the urge to check social media. "Speech in Dallas went really well," said Trump's Twitter feed, in a new post by @realDonaldTrump. The journalist looked over at the candidate, whose face was illuminated by the bright light of his phone.[44]

Were Brexit and Trump the product of a mismatch between elite discourse and the populist movements in the UK and the US? In the case of Brexit, Cameron would not have risked calling a referendum had he anticipated the result. He believed he would win it decisively. If politics were operating rationally, then voters would be persuaded by arguments about the economic benefits of continued EU membership and the risks of leaving. Cameron's campaign encouraged the opposition to raise the issue of immigration, believing they would look retrograde and extreme if they did so. Instead, warnings of economic costs went unheeded and immigration rhetoric dominated the debate.

In addressing themselves to Donald Trump, political, media, and academic elites found they did not speak his language and consistently underestimated his chances. The list of actions taken or not taken in 2016, leading to Trump's victory, is long. GOP elites failed to coalesce behind an opponent to Trump, assuming he was unelectable and would self-destruct anyway. The media, witnessing one should-be-campaign-ending scandal after another from Trump, repeatedly pronounced him finished, and yet he carried on. Poll aggregation methods, designed to extrapolate from multiple opinion polls and predict the final result, gave Trump long odds. Hillary Clinton, relying on the polling and her own data analytics, spent her time campaigning in long-shot red states, believing she was on the verge of a landslide rather than a narrow defeat. The Obama administration, discovering Russian interference in the campaign, downplayed it in public, thinking Hillary would win and the problem could be dealt with after the election.[45] The director of the FBI, James Comey, dismissed concerns about Trump campaign links with Russia while publicly announcing, days before the election, that he had reopened a probe into Clinton's use of a private email server. He, too, was operating on the assumption that she would be president and he must appear to be independent of her.

These are failures of interpretation. The Donald Trump of *The Apprentice* was a character that did not fit in politics as interpreted in *The West Wing*, *House of Cards*, or the other screen fictions studied here. And professional analysts, informed by political science models, did little better than the fictioneers in grasping the Trump phenomenon.

At the beginning of this book I argued that nothing in the social world has meaning separate from an interpretation of it. *Imagining Politics* has charted how one interpretation of politics—as a predictable and utilitarian game, played by interchangeable and cynical political actors—has been built and transmitted through our technologies of disciplinary research, pedagogy, and popular culture. For many, this image became a taken-for-granted knowledge structure, each piece reinforcing the whole as the fictions and the science we have examined circulated and perpetuated it. It shaped how we saw politics and what outcomes we thought were likely.

Large swaths of the citizenry in the US and the UK came to find this politics as usual so profoundly alienating that an alternative to it—any alternative—seemed attractive. We were given a populism of the right, but if political meaning is truly fluid, then other possibilities—perhaps a consensual, compromise politics à la *Borgen*, or a populism of the left—are possible too.

Books are never finished, the saying goes; one simply decides, or is forced, to stop working on them. As I stop working on this one, Omarosa Manigault-Newman, a contestant on the first season of *The Apprentice* whom President Donald Trump hired and then fired as a White House assistant, is all over cable television making accusations against him. The two stars of *The Apprentice* took their love/hate TV relationship into the White House. Like Charlie Brooker and the pig's head/prime minister imbroglio, I have had to question whether we are living in a simulation. Let me conclude, though, with a more sober observation: If, as I have argued in these pages, political meaning is truly fluid, and if it is made at least in part by how we study politics and how we portray it in popular culture, then we must continue to turn a critical eye to our fictions and to our discipline. Studying one and not the other threatens to leave us without the vocabulary we need to think and talk about our politics.

Notes

1. Excellent histories of the shifting interpretations of US politics offered by political science are Terrence Ball, "An Ambivalent Alliance" and "American Political Science," John S. Dryzek, "Revolutions without Enemies," John Gunnell, *Imagining the American Polity*, and David M. Ricci, *The Tragedy of Political Science*.

2. Though not all. There is a burgeoning literature on politics and popular culture. Particularly influential in the thinking behind this book have been Barry Buzan, "America in Space"; Renee Cramer, *Pregnant with the Stars*; Jeffrey R. Dudas, *Raised Right*; J. Furman Daniel III and Paul Musgrave, "Synthetic Experiences"; Lilly J. Goren and Linda Beail, *Mad Men and Politics*; Jonathan Grayson, Matt Davies, and Simon Philpott, "Pop Goes IR"; Iver B. Neumann and Daniel H. Nexon, "Harry Potter"; Trevor Parry-Giles and Shawn J. Parry-Giles, *The Prime Time Presidency*; Liesbet Van Zoonen, *Entertaining the Citizen*; Jutta Weldes, "Going Cultural: *Star Trek*, State Action, and Popular Culture."

3. Aaron Sorkin and David Brooks, "What's Character?"

4. Charles Taylor's essay "Interpretation and the Sciences of Man" is a crucial underpinning of this line of argument.

5. Trump called these elites "the swamp." I am assessing here only the political pitch he made in his campaign, not his subsequent actions as president.

6. Ricci, *Tragedy*; Donald Green and Ian Shapiro, *Pathologies of Rational Choice Theory*.

7. The necessary disclaimer here is that this is the briefest of distillations of a vibrant and sprawling intellectual tradition, one that is now institutionalized in the academic field of television studies. Excellent brief introductions can be found in Robert C. Allen, "Frequently Asked Questions"; Bernadette Casey et al., *Television Studies: The Key Concepts*; Jonathan Gray and Amanda D. Lotz, *Television Studies*; Ron Lembo, *Thinking through Television*.

8. John Fiske, *Television Culture*; John Fiske and John Hartley, *Reading Television*; David Morley, "Texts, Readers, Subjects"; David Morley, *Television, Audiences, and Cultural Studies*.

9. Thus the field of television studies is associated with the interpretive approach to knowledge. See Paul Rabinow and William M. Sullivan, "The Interpretive Turn: A Second Look," and Charles Taylor, "Interpretation and the Sciences of Man."

10. Stuart Hall, "Cultural Studies and the Center: Some Problematics and Problems"; Morley, *Television, Audiences, and Cultural Studies*.

11. Umberto Eco, "Toward a Semiotic Inquiry into the Television Message," 3–19.

12. Stuart Hall, "Encoding and Decoding in the Television Discourse"; Morley, "Texts, Readers, Subjects."

13. Hall, "Encoding and Decoding." Hall's contributions, of course, went significantly beyond the study of television.

14. Charles K. Atkin, John P. Murray, and Oguz B. Nayman, "The Surgeon General's Research Program on Television and Social Behavior," 22.

15. Hall, "Encoding and Decoding," 7.

16. Mikhail Bakhtin quoted in Jutta Weldes, "High Politics and Low Data."

17. Louis Althusser, "Ideology and Idological State Apparatuses"; Roland Barthes, *Mythologies*; Charlotte Brunsdon et al., *Feminist Television Criticism*.

18. Aspects of this argument are made in two compelling and important interventions: Patrick Thaddeus Jackson, "Making Sense of Making Sense," and Oren, "Political Science as History."

19. Waltz, *Theory of International Politics*, 8–9; Jon Elster, *Nuts and Bolts for the Social Sciences*.

20. What Thomas Kuhn, referring to the needs of all disciplines, called a "paradigm." Kuhn, *The Structure of Scientific Revolutions*, esp. 23–51.

21. This is a line of argument developed most thoroughly by David M. Ricci in *The Tragedy of Political Science*.

22. For extended histories of the development of these lines of thought in US political science, see Ricci, *Tragedy*; David Easton, "Political Science in the United States"; James Farr and Raymond Seidelman, "General Introduction"; Raymond Seidelman and Edward J. Harpham, *Disenchanted Realists*; Ball, "American Political Science"; Dorothy Ross, "The Development of the Social Sciences."

23. Any mainstream text of positivist political science methods will recount these principles. See Peregrine Schwartz-Shea and Dvora Yanow, "'Reading 'Methods' Texts.'" Classic statements are Gary King, Robert Keohane, and Sidney Verba, *Designing Social Inquiry*; and Elster, *Nuts and Bolts*.

24. David Easton, *The Political System*; Robert A. Dahl, "The Behavioral Approach in Political Science"; Ricci, *Tragedy*, 150–155; Seidelman and Harpham, *Disenchanted Realists*.

25. Easton, "Political Science."

26. Elster, *Nuts and Bolts*, offers a clear summary, esp. 22–29.

27. An alternative to the term "vocabulary" here is "web of meaning." Clifford M. Geertz, *The Interpretation of Cultures*.

CHAPTER TWO

1. Neustadt quoted in Charles O. Jones, "Scholar-Activist as Guardian."

2. *The West Wing*, season 2, episode 22, "Two Cathedrals."

3. Richard E. Neustadt, *Presidential Power and the Modern Presidents*, 4.

4. R. Neustadt, *Presidential Power*, 230.

5. R. Neustadt, *Presidential Power*, 131.

6. R. Neustadt, *Presidential Power*, 139.

7. Regrettably, as an empirical matter, all US presidents have been male, so I use male pronouns in most instances here.

8. R. Neustadt, *Presidential Power*, 50–55.

9. R. Neustadt, *Presidential Power*, 84.

10. R. Neustadt, *Presidential Power*, 4.

11. Charles O. Jones, "Richard E. Neustadt: Public Servant as Scholar," 5.

12. C. Jones, "Scholar-Activist," 36–37.

13. Elizabeth A. Neustadt, "Afterword: A Personal Reminiscence," 172.

14. E. Neustadt, "Afterword," 173.

15. R. Neustadt, *Presidential Power*, xvi.

16. Jonathan Alter, "Was Neustadt a Journalist, Too?," 105

17. R. Neustadt, *Presidential Power*, xxi.

18. Alter, "Was Neustadt a Journalist?," 104.

19. R. Neustadt, *Presidential Power*, xxi.

20. Alter, "Was Neustadt a Journalist?," 95.

21. John Podhoretz, "The Liberal Imagination."

22. Quoted in James Dyer, "The Definitive History of *The West Wing*."

23. *The West Wing*, season 1, episode 1, "Pilot."

24. John E. O'Connor and Peter C. Rollins, "Introduction," 10.

25. Patrick Finn, "*The West Wing*'s Textual President."

26. *The West Wing*, season 3, episode 10, "H. Con-172."

27. *The West Wing*, season 1, episode 19, "Let Bartlet Be Bartlet."

28. *The West Wing*, season 2, episode 13, "Bartlet's Third State of the Union."

29. *The West Wing*, season 1, episode 9, "The Short List."

30. *The West Wing*, season 1, episode 16, "20 Hours in LA."

31. *The West Wing*, season 1, episode 19, "Let Bartlet Be Bartlet."

32. *The West Wing*, season 2, episode 5, "And It's Surely to Their Credit."

33. *The West Wing*, season 2, episode 11, "The Leadership Breakfast."

34. *The West Wing*, season 1, episode 2, "Post Hoc, Ergo Propter Hoc."

35. *The West Wing*, season 1, episode 4, "Five Votes Down."

36. *The West Wing*, season 4, episode 1, "20 Hours in America."

37. Pamela Ezell, "The Sincere Sorkin White House."

38. Gary King, "The Methodology of Presidential Research."

39. King, "Methodology," 405–406.

40. Terry M. Moe, "Presidents, Institutions, and Theory," 379.

41. Terry M. Moe, "The Revolution in Presidential Studies," 701–704.

42. Moe, "Presidents, Institutions," 356.

43. Kenneth R. Mayer, *With the Stroke of a Pen*, 87.

44. Mayer, *With the Stroke*, 102.

45. William G. Howell, *Power without Persuasion*.

46. *The West Wing*, season 1, episode 7, "The State Dinner."

47. *The West Wing*, season 3, episode 5, "War Crimes."

CHAPTER THREE

1. *House of Cards*, season 1, episode 13, "Chapter 13."
2. Michael Schneider, "*House of Cards*: Creator Beau Willimon on the D.C. Thriller's Second Season."
3. *House of Cards*, season 4, episode 6, "Chapter 45."
4. *House of Cards*, season 1, episode 1, "Chapter 1."
5. Zeke J. Miller, "Obama Wishes Washington Really Was Like *House of Cards*."
6. Joseph A. Schlesinger, *Ambition and Politics*, 12–16.
7. Schlesinger, *Ambition and Politics*, vii.
8. Schlesinger, *Ambition and Politics*, 10.
9. Gordon S. Black, "A Theory of Political Ambition."
10. We might locate ambition theory at the point where behavioralism intersects with rational choice theory, making Schlesinger's *Ambition and Politics* a foundational work of the scientific-rational consensus.
11. David R. Mayhew, *Congress: The Electoral Connection*, 6.
12. Schlesinger, *Ambition and Politics*, 209.
13. "Nine Things *House of Cards* Took from Shakespeare."
14. Ian Crouch, "Richard III's House of Cards."
15. *House of Cards*, season 1, episode 1, "Chapter 1."
16. *House of Cards*, season 3, episode 3, "Chapter 29."
17. *House of Cards*, season 4, episode 6, "Chapter 45."
18. Robert A. Caro, *A Master of the Senate*, 760.
19. Robert A. Caro, *The Path to Power*, 200.
20. Caro, *Path to Power*, 100.
21. Robert A. Caro, *Means of Ascent*, 141.
22. Caro, *Master of the Senate*, xvi.
23. Underwood, too, is portrayed as a poor public speaker and an average debater in *House of Cards*; his talents lie in backroom arm-twisting.
24. Caro, *Master of the Senate*, xviii.
25. Caro, *Master of the Senate*, xxi.
26. Caro, *Master of the Senate*, 120–121.
27. Robert A. Caro, *The Passage of Power*, xviii.
28. Caro, *Master of the Senate*, 886.
29. Caro, *Master of the Senate*.
30. Caro, *Passage to Power*, 307–339.
31. *House of Cards*, season 1, episode 13, "Chapter 13."
32. Caro, *Means of Ascent*, 141.
33. Caro, *Passage of Power*, 87.
34. *House of Cards*, season 2, episode 13, "Chapter 26."

CHAPTER FOUR

1. In reconstructing the Hanover Inn press conference, I relied upon Richard Ben Cramer, *What It Takes: The Way to the White House*, 466–69; Matt Bai, *All the Truth Is Out*, 147–56; and Paul Taylor, *See How They Run*, 50–53.

2. Bai, *All the Truth*, 70.

3. Taylor, *See How They Run*, 25–27.

4. Taylor, *See How They Run*, 9.

5. Jon Margolis, "Hart Takes on the Press, Blasts Tryst Story as False."

6. Taylor, *See How They Run*, 51, 25.

7. Taylor, *See How They Run*, 51–52.

8. Bai, *All the Truth*, 20

9. Bai, *All the Truth*, 158–59.

10. Matt Bai, "The Outsider."

11. Bai, *All the Truth*, 181.

12. Bai, *All the Truth*, xiv, xv.

13. Sarah Hughes, "Shonda Rhimes: Meet the Most Powerful Woman in U.S. Television."

14. Willa Paskin, "Network TV Is Broken. So How Does Shonda Rhimes Keep Making Hits?"

15. Todd Van Der Werff, "How *Scandal* Became the Perfect Distillation of America's Political Nightmares."

16. Hughes, "Shonda Rhimes."17. Brendan Nyhan, "Strategic Outrage: The Politics of Presidential Scandal"; Charles M. Cameron, "Studying the Polarized Presidency," 655.

18. Nyhan, "Strategic Outrage," 25.

19. Nyhan, "Strategic Outrage," 56, 78.

20. Benjamin Ginsberg and Martin Shefter, *Politics by Other Means*.

21. Paul J. Quirk, "Coping with the Politics of Scandal," 901–902.

22. Quoted in Stanley A. Renshon, "The Public's Response to the Clinton Scandals," 174.

23. Regina G. Lawrence and W. Lance Bennett, "Rethinking Media Politics and Public Opinion: Reactions to the Clinton-Lewinsky Scandal," 425.

24. Arthur H. Miller, "Sex, Politics, and Public Opinion," 723.

25. Miller, "Sex, Politics, and Public Opinion, 724.

26. Miller, "Sex, Politics, and Public Opinion, 725–26.

27. Lawrence and Bennett, "Rethinking Media Politics," 432.

28. Laura Stoker, "Judging Presidential Character: The Demise of Gary Hart."

29. Judy Smith, *Good Self, Bad Self: How to Bounce Back from a Personal Crisis*.

30. Tom Fiedler, "Did the Gary Hart Scandal Really Ruin Politics?"

31. Taylor, *See How They Run*, 10–11.

32. Seymour M. Hersh, *The Dark Side of Camelot*.

33. Larry J. Sabato, *Feeding Frenzy: Attack Journalism and American Politics*, 61–62.

34. See Bai, *All the Truth*, 66.

35. Cramer, *What It Takes: The Way to the White House*, loc. 13861. See also Sabato, *Feeding Frenzy*, 64–68.

36. Gail Sheehy, "The Road to Bimini."

37. Nyhan, "Strategic Outrage," 2.

38. Bai, *All the Truth*, 6.

39. To say Barber was driven by a different interpretation of politics than the scientific-rational mainstream of political science is not to say his interpretation is more correct or even more useful. Even others who accepted Barber's major

intervention—that character matters—found significant fault with his work. See Alexander L. George, "Assessing Presidential Character."

40. James David Barber, *Presidential Character*, 3–4.

41. Barber, *Presidential Character*, 14.

42. Barber, *Presidential Character*, 441.

43. Taylor, *See How They Run*, 77–78.

44. Taylor, *See How They Run*, 60.

CHAPTER FIVE

1. Kingsley, *How to Be Danish*, loc. 113.

2. This implicates Althusser's notion of the Ideological State Apparatus (ISA)—a set of institutions that reproduces the ideology of the state in order to ensure the perpetuation of existing power relations—a model that posits dark motives on the part of the state elite. The admiring version of Danishness elaborated in this chapter perhaps betrays the naïveté of an outsider (although I note the significant challenges posed to it by globalization and migration). Althusser's ISA model seems a good conceptual framework for thinking about the technologies that generate and perpetuate "Danishness" via, as I address in this chapter, the myth-making project of N. S. Grundtvig and his followers. Althusser, though, sees the ISA as the cultural arm of the coercive institutions of the state in perpetuating the exploitation of workers under capitalism, which pushes the argument in a more sinister direction than that advanced by the Danish scholars on whom I draw in this chapter.

3. Vicky Frost, "Adam Price: The Chef Who Cooked Up *Borgen*."

4. David Gritten, "*Borgen*: Sidse Babett Knudsen Interview."

5. Lauren Collins, "Danish Postmodern."

6. Collins, "Danish Postmodern."

7. Jade Bremner, "Revealed: The Real *Borgen*."

8. Frost, "Adam Price."

9. Chris Wodskou, "*Borgen* Creator: Coalition Governments Shouldn't Be Seen as Some Kind of Weakness."

10. Giovanni Sartori, *Parties and Party Systems: A Framework for Analysis*.

11. John L. Campbell and John A. Hall, "The State of Denmark," 28–29.

12. Hjalte Rasmussen, "Constitutional Laxity and International High Economic Performance: Is There a Nexus?," 204.

13. Rasmussen, "Constitutional Laxity," 239.

14. Arend Liphjart, *Patterns of Democracy: Government Forms and Performance in 38 Countries*.

15. Knud J. V. Jespersen, *A History of Denmark*, loc. 1673.

16. Robert Kuttner, "The Copenhagen Consensus: Reading Adam Smith in Denmark."

17. Ove K. Pedersen, "Corporatism and Beyond: The Negotiated Democracy."

18. Kuttner, "Copenhagen Consensus." 80.

19. Campbell and Hall, "State of Denmark," 13–14.

20. Kingsley, *How to Be Danish*, loc. 798, 802.

21. Jespersen, *History of Denmark*, loc 3977.

22. Uffe Ostergard, "Denmark: A Big Small State—The Peasant Roots of Danish Modernity," 71.

23. Ostergard, "Denmark: A Big Small State," 76–82.

24. Ostergard, "Denmark: A Big Small State," 91.

25. Lijphart, *Patterns of Democracy*, 91–104.

26. William A. Riker, *The Theory of Political Coalitions*.

27. Alan Ware, *Political Parties and Party Systems*, 330–42.

28. Ian Budge and Michael Laver, "The Policy Basis of Government Coalitions."

29. Anthony Downs, *An Economic Theory of Democracy*.

30. Ian Budge and Michael Laver, "Office-Seeking and Policy Pursuit in Coalition Theory."

31. *Borgen*, season 1, episode 7, "See No Evil, Speak No Evil."

32. Collins, "Danish Postmodern."

33. Chris Wimpress, "*Borgen* Creator Adam Price Talks Work-Life Balance, Danish Politics, and Cameron's Mention."

34. Eric S. Einhorn and John Logue, "Can Welfare States Be Sustained in a Global Economy? Lessons from Scandinavia" 7–8.

35. Einhorn and Logue, "Can Welfare States Be Sustained?," 10–14.

36. Suzanne Daley, "Danes Rethink Welfare State Generous to a Fault."

37. Robert H. Cox, "The Social Construction of an Imperative: Why Welfare Reform Happened in Denmark and the Netherlands but Not in Germany."

38. Christopher Caldwell, "Islam on the Outskirts of the Welfare State."

39. Bo Lidegaard, "Denmark's Far-Right Kingmakers."

40. Edward Delman, "How Not to Welcome Refugees."

41. Russell, "Living Danishly," loc. 3234.

42. Lidegaard, "Denmark's Far-Right Kingmakers."

CHAPTER SIX

1. Sketch available here: https://www.youtube.com/watch?v=cwaX_DgHZkM, accessed 8/20/2017.

2. Quoted in Graham McCann, *A Very Courageous Decision: The Inside Story of Yes, Minister*, loc. 4237.

3. Jonathan Lynn, *Comedy Rules: From the Cambridge Footlights to Yes, Minister*, loc. 2065.

4. Lynn, *Comedy Rules*, loc. 2065.

5. This is a broadly congruent, yet slightly darker reading of *Yes, Minister* than that given by John Street: "The joke is not that funny things happen in politics, but that politics is laughable." Quoted in Liesbet van Zoonen, *Entertaining the Citizen: When Politics and Popular Culture Converge*, 114.

6. Lynn, *Comedy Rules*, loc. 1079.

7. McCann, *Very Courageous Decision*, loc. 2739.

8. McCann, *Very Courageous Decision*, loc. 671.

9. Lynn, *Comedy Rules*, loc. 1233.

10. Lynn, *Comedy Rules*, loc. 31.

11. Lynn, *Comedy Rules*, loc. 1289.

12. Richard Crossman, *The Diaries of a Cabinet Minister*, 23–25.

13. McCann, *Very Courageous Decision*, loc 785.

14. Leslie Chapman, *Your Disobedient Servant*, 51

15. Chapman, *Your Disobedient Servant*, 46–47.

16. Chapman, *Your Disobedient Servant* , 95.

17. Chapman, *Your Disobedient Servant* 11–12.

18. Chapman, *Your Disobedient Servant* , 41–42.

19. Chapman, *Your Disobedient Servant*, 59–60.

20. McCann, *Very Courageous Decision*, loc. 878.

21. Lynn, *Comedy Rules*, loc. 1539.

22. "The Bed of Nails"—a line borrowed from American journalist James Reston: "The ship of state is the only known vessel which leaks from the top."

23. McCann, *Very Courageous Decision*, loc. 2515.

24. *Yes, Minister*, season 2, episode 4, "The Greasy Pole."

25. *Yes, Minister*, season 3, episode 3, "The Skeleton in the Cupboard."

26. *Yes, Prime Minister*, season 2, episode 6, "The Patron of the Arts."

27. *Yes, Minister*, season 2, episode 3, "The Death List."

28. *Yes, Prime Minister*, season 2, episode 5, "Power to the People."

29. *Yes, Prime Minister*, season 2, episode 5, "Power to the People."

30. *Yes, Minister*, season1, episode 5, "The Writing on the Wall."

31. *Yes, Minister*, season1, episode 6, "The Right to Know."

32. *Yes, Minister*, season 3, episode 1, "Equal Opportunities."

33. *Yes, Minister*, season 3, episode 6, "The Whisky Priest."

34. *Yes, Minister*, season 1, episode 6, "The Right to Know."

35. *Yes, Minister*, season 1, episode 6, "The Right to Know."

36. *Yes, Minister*, season 2, episode 6, "The Quality of Life."

37. *Yes, Prime Minister*, season 2, episode 1, "The Grand Design."

38. I owe much of the structure of the argument in this section to the discussion in Kenneth A. Shepsle and Mark S. Bonchek, *Analyzing Politics: Rationality, Behavior, and Institutions*, 345–79.

39. Steve H. Hanke, "William A. Niskanen: In Memoriam."

40. Gary A. Miller and Terry M. Moe, "Bureaucrats, Legislators, and the Size of Government."

41. Shepsle and Bonchek, *Analyzing Politics*, 360–68.

42. Mathew G. McCubbins, Roger G. Noll, and Barry R. Weingast, "Administrative Procedures as Instruments of Political Control."

43. "The Bed of Nails (*Yes Minister*), Wikipedia, https://en.wikipedia.org/wiki/The_Bed_of_Nails_(*Yes_Minister*).

44. McCann, *Very Courageous Decision*, loc 6955.

45. Lynn, *Comedy Rules*.

46. McCann, *Very Courageous Decision*, loc 6438.

CHAPTER SEVEN

1. This account of the Jo Moore affair draws upon the House of Commons, Public Administration Select Committee report "'These Unfortunate Events': Lessons of Recent Events at the Former DTLR," and Peter Oborne and Simon Walters, *Alastair Campbell*, 282–84.

2. Jonathan Carr-Brown, "Byers 'Lied' over Press Chief's Resignation."

3. Political operatives who attach themselves to candidates and elected officials, and are consumed with media spin, are a US invention that was copied by UK politicians. While there were earlier precedents, the Clinton '92 war room of James Carville, Paul Begala, and George Stephanopoulos brought the species to widespread notoriety. See Chris Hegedus and D. A. Pennebaker's *The War Room*, a documentary much watched by the rising Labour Party politicians Tony Blair and Gordon Brown.

4. Captured in key works of the period such as Francis Fukuyama, *The End of History*; Anthony Giddens, *The Third Way*; and Thomas Friedman, *The Lexus and the Olive Tree*.

5. BBC Press Office, "Interview with Armando Iannucci."

6. Margaret Scammell, "Politics and Image."

7. *The Thick of It*, season 1, episode 3.

8. *The Thick of It*, season 2, episode 3.

9. *The Thick of It*, season 3, episode 3.

10. *The Thick of It*, season 4, episode 6.

11. *The Thick of It*, season 3, episode 2.

12. *The Thick of It*, season 4, episode 2.

13. *The Thick of It*, season 4, episode 1.

14. *The Thick of It*, season 3, episode 1.

15. *The Thick of It*, season 2, episode 1.

16. *The Thick of It*, season 1, episode 1.

17. *The Thick of It*, season 4, episode 6.

18. Eamonn Forde, "Armando Iannucci Interview."

19. London School of Economics GV314 Group, "New Life at the Top," 3. Liesbet van Zoonen analyzes politics in the age of the spin doctor less as farce than as soap opera. See van Zoonen, *Entertaining the Citizen*, 19–36.

20. Stuart Jeffries, "Now Is Not the Time for a Crap Opposition."

21. Tony Blair, *A Journey: My Political Life*, 9.

22. Oborne and Walters, *Alastair Campbell*, 197.

23. Oborne and Walters, *Alastair Campbell*, 153.

24. Oborne and Walters, *Alastair Campbell*, 138.

25. Oborne and Walters, *Alastair Campbell*, 234.

26. Oonagh Gay and Paul Fawcett, *Special Advisors*, 43.

27. Oborne and Walters, *Alastair Campbell*, 156–61.

28. Oborne and Walters, *Alastair Campbell*, 156.

29. Oborne and Walters, *Alastair Campbell*, 139–40.

30. Nicholas Jones, *Sultans of Spin*, 186–88.

31. Margaret Cook, *A Slight and Delicate Creature*.

32. Oborne and Walters, *Alastair Campbell*, 332–37.

33. "Full Transcript of Gilligan's 'Sexed Up' Broadcast,"

34. Oborne and Walters, *Alastair Campbell*, 332–33.

35. Channel 4 News, "Alastair Campbell Interview."

36. Oborne and Walters, *Alastair Campbell*, 336–37.

37. On Dr. Kelly, see Oborne and Walters, *Alastair Campbell*, 338–47.

38. Lacey Rose, "Julia-Louis Dreyfus Reveals Awkward Fan Letter from Hillary."

39. *The Thick of It*, season 4, episode 6.

CHAPTER EIGHT

1. Edward Luce, *The Retreat of Western Liberalism*.

2. See Cas Mudde and Cristobal Rovira Kaltwasser, *Populism: A Very Short Introduction*; John Judis, *The Populist Explosion: How the Great Recession Transformed American and European Politics*. The populisms of Brexit and Trump were right-wing, nationalistic populisms. Left-wing analogues also rose during this period of time. Bernie Sanders, running as an independent and social democrat, challenged centrist Hillary Clinton for the Democratic party nomination and performed far better than the political class, operating within their suddenly useless web of meaning, had expected. Similarly, Jeremy Corbyn, a serial rebel and apparently unelectable extremist parliamentarian of the British Labour Party, captured the party leadership and, in the 2017 general election, denied the Conservative Party an overall majority. Corbyn's success had similarly been missed by British political scientists.

3. Elle Hunt, "Armando Iannucci on Why He's Glad He Left *Veep*: 'I Don't Know How I'd Respond to America Now.'"

4. *Black Mirror*, season 2, episode 3, "The Waldo Moment."

5. Nicholas Kristof, "My Shared Shame: The Media Helped Make Trump."

6. Ian Schwartz, "Cokie Roberts vs. Donald Trump on Offensive Language."

7. May Bulman, "Former Mexican President Vicente Fox Tells Donald Trump's Administration: We're Not Paying for the F**cking Wall."

8. Louis Jacobson and Manuela Tobias, "Has Donald Trump 'Never Promoted or Encouraged Violence,' as Sarah Huckerbee Sanders said?"

9. Ashley Parker, "Covering Donald Trump, Witnessing the Danger Up Close."

10. Dyson, "Cognitive Style."

11. This account of the Brexit campaign relies heavily on Alex Spence, "David Cameron Unleashes Project Fear," and Rachel Behr, "How Remain Failed: The Inside Story of a Doomed Campaign."

12. BBC Radio 4, "Any Questions?" June 25, 2016.

13. Heather Stewart and Rowena Mason, "Nigel Farage's Anti-Migrant Poster Reported to Police."

14. Raphael Behr, "How Remain Failed: The Inside Story of a Doomed Campaign."

15. Tom McTague, Alex Spence, and Edward-Isaac Dovere, "How David Cameron Blew It."

16. Behr, "How Remain Failed."

17. Matt Taibbi, *Insane Clown President*, loc. 2628.

18. "Pushback," *The Economist*, March 5, 2016.

19. Marty Cohen, David Karol, Hans Noll, and John Zaller, *The Party Decides: Presidential Nominations Before and After Reform*, 12, 32–36.

20. Cohen et al., *Party Decides*, 188–90.

21. Taibbi, *Insane Clown President*, loc. 107, 145.

22. Daniel Drezner, "My Very Peculiar and Speculative Theory of Why the GOP Has Not Stopped Donald Trump."

23. "Pushback."

24. Kelsey McKinney, "The Mythmaker."

25. Michael Kranish and Marc Fisher, "The Inside Story of How 'The Apprentice' Rescued Donald Trump."

26. Kranish and Fisher, "Inside Story."

27. "Killer streets" is Trump's phrase, from season 1, episode 1 of *The Apprentice*.

28. Kranish and Fisher, "Inside Story."

29. James Poniewozik, "The New Reality of TV: All Trump, All the Time."

30. Rick Perlstein, "I Thought I Understood the American Right."

31. *The Apprentice*, season 1, episode 3, "Respect."

32. Kranish and Fisher, "Inside Story."

33. *The Apprentice*, season 1, episode 1, "Meet the Billionaire."

34. NPR, "'Hillbilly Elegy' Recalls a Childhood Where 'Poverty Was 'The Family Tradition.'"

35. Michael Ashcroft and Isabel Oakeshott, "British Prime Minister and an Obscene Act with a Pig's Head."

36. Todd Van Der Werff, "*Black Mirror* Season 3 Review."

37. Van Der Werff, "*Black Mirror* Season 3 Review."

38. Katharine Viner, "How Technology Disrupted the Truth."

39. US Department of Justice, "USA v. Internet Research Agency LLC et al."

40. Gregor Aisch, Jon Huang, and Cecelia Kang, "Dissecting the So-Called #Pizzagate Conspiracy Theories."

41. Michael C. Lynch, *The Internet of Us*.

42. Viner, "How Technology Disrupted the Truth."

43. Taibbi, *Insane Clown President*, loc. 2240.

44. Mark Leibovich, "Donald Trump Is Not Going Anywhere."

45. Greg Miller, Ellen Nakashimi, and Adam Entous, "Obama's Secret Struggle to Punish Putin for Russia's Election Interference."

References

Aisch, Gregor, Jon Huang, and Cecelia Kang. "Dissecting the So-Called #Pizzagate Conspiracy Theories." *New York Times*, December 10, 2016. https://www.nytimes.com/interactive/2016/12/10/business/media/pizzagate.html.

Allen, Robert C. "Frequently Asked Questions: A General Introduction to the Reader." In *The Television Studies Reader*, edited by Robert C. Allen and Annette Hill, 1–60. London: Routledge, 2004.

Alter, Jonathan. "Was Neustadt a Journalist, Too?" In Dickinson and Neustadt, *Guardian of the Presidency*, 94–105.

Althusser, Louis. "Ideology and Ideological State Apparatuses." In *Essays on Ideology*. London, UK: Verso, 1976, 1–60.

Ashcroft, Michael, and Isabel Oakeshott. "British Prime Minister and an Obscene Act with a Pig's Head." *Daily Mail*, September 20, 2015. http://www.dailymail.co.uk/news/article-3242550/Cameron-pig-bemused-look-face-future-PM-took-outrageous-initiation-ceremony-joining-Oxford-dining-society.html.

Atkin, Charles K., John P. Murray, and Oguz B. Nayman. "The Surgeon General's Research Program on Television and Social Behavior: A Review of Empirical Findings." *Journal of Broadcasting* 16, no. 1 (1977):21–35.

Bai, Matt. *All the Truth Is Out: The Week Politics Went Tabloid*. New York: Vintage, 2015.

Bai, Matt. "The Outsider." *New York Times Magazine*, February 2, 2003.

Ball, Terrence. "An Ambivalent Alliance: Political Science and American Democracy." In *Political Science in History: Research Programs and Political Traditions*, edited by James Farr, John S. Dryzek, and Stephen T. Leonard, 41–65. New York: Cambridge University Press, 1995.

Ball, Terrence. "American Political Science in Its Postwar Political Context." In Farr and Seidelman, *Discipline and History*, 207–222.

Barber, James David. *Presidential Character: Predicting Performance in the White House*. New York: Taylor & Francis, 2009.

Barthes, Roland. *Mythologies*. New York: Hill & Wang, 2013.

BBC Press Office. "Interview with Armando Iannucci." August 8, 2005. http://www.bbc.co.uk/pressoffice/pressreleases/stories/2005/12_december/08/thick_armando.shtml.

BBC Radio 4. "Any Questions?" June 25, 2016. http://www.bbc.co.uk/programmes/b07glx85.

Behr, Raphael. "How Remain Failed: The Inside Story of a Doomed Campaign." *The Guardian*, July 5, 2016. https://www.theguardian.com/politics/2016/jul/05/how-remain-failed-inside-story-doomed-campaign.

Black, Gordon S. "A Theory of Political Ambition: Career Choices and the Role of Structural Incentives." *American Political Science Review* 66, no. 1 (1972): 144–59.

Blair, Tony. *A Journey: My Political Life*. New York: Knopf, 2010.

Blyth, Mark. "Great Punctuations: Prediction, Randomness, and the Evolution of Comparative Political Science." *American Political Science Review* 100 (2006): 493–98.

Bremner, Jade. "Revealed: The Real *Borgen*." *Radio Times*. April 2, 2012. http://www.radiotimes.com/news/2012-02-04/revealed-the-real-borgen.

Brunsdon, Charlotte, Julie D'Acci, and Lynn Spigel, eds. *Feminist Television Criticism: A Reader*. Oxford: Oxford University Press, 1997.

Budge, Ian, and Michael Laver. "Office Seeking and Policy Pursuit in Coalition Theory." *Legislative Studies Quarterly* 11, no. 4 (1986): 484–506.

Budge, Ian, and Michael Laver. "The Policy Basis of Government Coalitions: A Comparative Investigation." *British Journal of Political Science* 23, no. 4 (1993): 499–519.

Bulman, May. "Former Mexican President Vicente Fox Tells Donald Trump's Administration: We're Not Paying for the Fcking Wall." *The Independent*, January 26, 2017. http://www.independent.co.uk/news/world/americas/former-mexican-president-name-donald-trump-mexico-border-wall-were-not-paying-for-the-f-wall-enrique-a7546696.html.

Buzan, Barry. "America in Space: The International Relations of Star Trek and Battlestar Galactica." *Millenium* 39, no. 1 (2010): 175–80.

Caldwell, Christopher. "Islam on the Outskirts of the Welfare State." *New York Times Magazine*, February 5, 2006. http://www.nytimes.com/2006/02/05/magazine/islam-on-the-outskirts-of-the-welfare-state.html.

Cameron, Charles M. "Studying the Polarized Presidency." *Presidential Studies Quarterly* 32, no. 4 (2002): 647–63.

Campbell, John L., and John A. Hall. "The State of Denmark." In Campbell, Hall, and Pedersen, *National Identity and the Varieties of Capitalism*, 1–51.

Campbell, John L., John A. Hall, and Ove K. Petersen. *National Identity and the Varieties of Capitalism: The Danish Experience*. Montreal: McGill-Queen's University Press, 2006.

Caro, Robert A. *Master of the Senate*. New York: Vintage, 2002.

Caro, Robert A. *Means of Ascent*. New York: Vintage, 1990.

Caro, Robert A. *The Passage of Power*. New York: Vintage, 2012.

Caro, Robert A. *The Path to Power*. New York: Vintage, 1982.

Carr-Brown, Jonathan. "Byers 'Lied' over Press Chief's Resignation." *Sunday Times*, February 24, 2002.

Casey, Bernadette, Neil Casey, Ben Calvert, Liam French, and Justin Lewis. *Television Studies: The Key Concepts*. New York, Routledge, 2008.

Chapman, Leslie. *Your Disobedient Servant*. London: Chatto & Windus, 1978.

Channel 4 News. "Alastair Campbell Interview." June 27, 2003. http://www.channel4.com/news/articles/politics/domestic_politics/exclusive%2balastair%2bcampbell%2binterview/262148.html.

Cohen, Marty, David Karol, Hans Noll, and John Zaller. *The Party Decides: Presidential Nominations Before and After Reform*. Chicago: Chicago University Press, 2008.

Collins, Lauren. "Danish Postmodern." *New Yorker*, January 7, 2013. https://www.newyorker.com/magazine/2013/01/07/danish-postmodern.

Converse, Phillip E. "Researching Electoral Politics." *American Political Science Review* 100 (2006): 605–612.

Cook, Margaret. *A Slight and Delicate Creature*. London: Weidenfeld & Nicolson, 1999.

Cox, Robert H. "The Social Construction of an Imperative: Why Welfare Reform Happened in Denmark and the Netherlands but Not in Germany." *World Politics* 53 (2001): 463–98.

Cramer, Renee Ann. *Pregnant with the Stars: Watching and Wanting the Celebrity Baby Bump*. Stanford, CA: Stanford University Press, 2015.

Cramer, Richard Ben. *What It Takes: The Way to the White House*. New York: Random House, 1990. Kindle.

Crossman, Richard. *The Diaries of a Cabinet Minister*. London: Henry Holt, 1976.

Crouch, Ian. "Richard III's House of Cards." *New Yorker*, February 4, 2013. http://www.newyorker.com/culture/culture-desk/richard-iiis-house-of-cards.

Dahl, Robert A. "The Behavioral Approach in Political Science: Epitaph for a Monument to a Successful Protest." *American Political Science Review* 55 (1961): 763–72.

Daley, Suzanne. "Danes Rethink Welfare State Generous to a Fault." *New York Times*, April 20, 2013. http://www.nytimes.com/2013/04/21/world/europe/danes-rethink-a-welfare-state-ample-to-a-fault.html.

Daniel, J. Furman III and Paul Musgrave, "Synthetic Experiences: How Popular Culture Matters for Images of International Relations" *International Studies Quarterly* 61, no. 3 (2017): 503–516.

Delman, Edward. "How Not to Welcome Refugees." *The Atlantic*, January 27, 2016. https://www.theatlantic.com/international/archive/2016/01/denmark-refugees-immigration-law/431520.

Dickinson, Matthew J., and Elizabeth A. Neustadt. *Guardian of the Presidency: The Legacy of Richard E. Neustadt*. Washington, DC: Brookings Institution Press, 2007.

Downs, Anthony. *An Economic Theory of Democracy*. New York: Harper & Row, 1957.

Drezner, Daniel. "My Very Peculiar and Speculative Theory of Why the GOP Has Not Stopped Donald Trump." *Washington Post*, February 23, 2016. https://www.washingtonpost.com/posteverything/wp/2016/02/23/my-very-peculiar-and-speculative-theory-of-why-the-gop-has-not-stopped-donald-trump/?utm_term=.f3ee41722b69.

Dryzek, John S. "Revolutions without Enemies: Key Transformations in Political Science" *American Political Science Review* 100, no. 4 (2006): 487–492.

Dudas, Jeffrey R. *Raised Right*. Stanford, CA: Stanford University Press, 2017.

Dyer, James. "The Definitive History of *The West Wing*." *Empire*. http://www.empireonline.com/west-wing/default.html.

Dyson. "Cognitive Style and Foreign Policy: Margaret Thatcher's Black-and-White Thinking." *International Political Science Review* 30, no. 1 (2009): 33–48.

Dyson, Stephen Benedict. *Otherworldly Politics: The International Relations of Star Trek, Game of Thrones, and Battlestar Galactica*. Baltimore: Johns Hopkins University Press, 2015.

Easton, David. "Political Science in the United States: Past and Present." In Farr and Seidelman, *Discipline and History*, 291–310.

Easton, David. *The Political System: An Inquiry into the State of Political Science.* New York: Knopf, 1953.

Eco, Umberto. "Toward a Semiotic Inquiry into the Television Message." In *Television: Critical Concepts in Media and Cultural Studies*, vol. 2, edited by Toby Miller, 3–19. New York: Taylor & Francis, 2003.

Ehrlichman, John. *The Company.* New York: Pocket, 1977.

Einhorn, Eric S., and John Logue. "Can Welfare States Be Sustained in a Global Economy? Lessons from Scandinavia." *Political Science Quarterly* 125, no. 1 (2010): 1–29.

Elster, Jon. *Nuts and Bolts for the Social Sciences.* New York: Cambridge University Press, 1989.

Ezell, Pamela. "The Sincere Sorkin White House; or, The Importance of Seeming Earnest." In Rollins and O'Connor, *The West Wing*, 159–74.

Farr, James. "Political Science and the State." In Farr and Seidelman, *Discipline and History*, 63–80.

Farr, James, and Raymond Seidelman, eds. *Discipline and History: Political Science in the United States.* Ann Arbor: University of Michigan Press, 1993.

Farr, James, and Raymond Seidelman. "General Introduction." In Farr and Seidelman, *Discipline and History*, 1–14.

Fiedler, Tom. "Did the Gary Hart Scandal Really Ruin Politics?" *Politico*, October 2, 2014. http://www.politico.com/magazine/story/2014/10/gary-hart-politics-111563.

Finn, Patrick. "*The West Wing*'s Textual President." In Rollins and O'Connor, *The West Wing*, 101–124.

Fiske, John. *Television Culture.* New York: Routledge, 1987.

Fiske, John, and John Hartley. *Reading Television.* New York: Routledge, 2003.

Forde, Eamonn. "Armando Iannucci." *The Big Issue*, April 20, 2015. https://www.bigissue.com/interviews/armando-iannucci-i-hope-thick-didnt-put-young-people-off-politics.

Friedman, Thomas. *The Lexus and the Olive Tree.* New York: Farrar, Straus, Giroux, 1999.

Frost, Vicky. "Adam Price: The Chef Who Cooked Up *Borgen*." *The Guardian*, January 30, 2013.

Fukuyama, Francis. *The End of History.* New York: Free Press, 1992.

"Full Transcript of Gilligan's 'Sexed Up' Broadcast." *The Guardian*, July 9, 2003. https://www.theguardian.com/media/2003/jul/09/Iraqandthemedia.bbc.

Gay, Oonagh, and Paul Fawcett. *Special Advisors.* London: House of Commons Library, 2005.

Geertz, Clifford M. *The Interpretation of Cultures.* New York: Basic Books, 1973.

George, Alexander L. "Assessing Presidential Character." *World Politics* 26, no. 2 (1974): 234–82.

Giddens, Anthony. *The Third Way: The Renewal of Social Democracy.* Cambridge, UK: Polity, 1999.

Ginsberg, Benjamin, and Martin Shefter. *Politics by Other Means.* New York: Basic Books, 1990.

Goren, Lilly J., and Linda Beail, eds. *Mad Men and Politics: Nostalgia and the Remaking of Modern America*. New York: Bloomsbury Academic, 2015.

Gray, Jonathan, and Amanda D. Lotz. *Television Studies*. Cambridge, UK: Polity, 2012.

Grayson, Kyle, Matt Davies, and Simon Philpott. "Pop Goes IR? Researching the Popular Culture-World Politics Continuum." *Politics* 29, no. 3 (2009): 155–63.

Green, Donald P., and Ian Shapiro. *Pathologies of Rational Choice Theory*. New Haven, CT: Yale University Press, 1994.

Gritten, David. "*Borgen*: Sidse Babett Knudsen Interview." *The Telegraph*, November 23, 2013. https://www.telegraph.co.uk/culture/tvandradio/10465576/Borgen-Sidse-Babett-Knudsen-interview.html.

Gunnell, John. *Imagining the American Polity*. University Park: Pennsylvania State University Press, 2004.

Hartz, Louis. *The Liberal Tradition in America*. New York: Harcourt, Brace & World, 1955.

Hall, Stuart. "Cultural Studies and the Centre: Some Problematics and Problems." In *Culture, Media, Language: Working Papers in Cultural Studies, 1972–79*, edited by Stuart Hall, Dorothy Hobson, Andrew Lowe, and Paul Willis. London: Routledge, 2003.

Hall, Stuart. "Encoding and Decoding in the Television Discourse." Working paper, Centre for Cultural Studies, University of Birmingham, 1973. http://www.birmingham.ac.uk/Documents/college-artslaw/history/cccs/stencilled-occasional-papers/1to8and11to24and38to48/SOP07.pdf.

Hall, Stuart. "Introduction to Media Studies at the Centre." In Hall, Hobson, Lowe, and Willis, *Culture, Media, Language*, 117–21.

Hall, Stuart, Dorothy Hobson, Andrew Lowe, and Paul Willis. *Culture, Media, Language: Working Papers in Cultural Studies, 1972–79*. New York: Routledge, 1996.

Hanke, Steve H. "William A. Niskanen: In Memoriam." *Cato.org*, January 4, 2012. https://www.cato.org/publications/commentary/william-niskanen-memoriam.

Hegedus, Chris, and D. A. Pennebaker. *The War Room*. Criterion Collection, 1992.

Hennessy, Peter. *Whitehall*. London: Pimlico, 2001.

Hersh, Seymour M. *The Dark Side of Camelot*. New York: Back Bay, 1998.

Hollis, Martin, and Steve Smith. *Explaining and Understanding International Relations*. New York: Oxford University Press, 1991.

Hopf, Ted. *Social Construction of International Politics*. Ithaca, NY: Cornell University Press, 1999.

Horkheimer, Max, and Theodor W. Adorno. *Dialectic of Enlightenment*. Stanford, CA: Stanford University Press, 2007.

House of Commons, Public Administration Select Committee. "'These Unfortunate Events': Lessons of Recent Events at the Former DTLR." Eighth Report of Session 2001–02. London: House of Commons, July 19, 2002. https://publications.parliament.uk/pa/cm200102/cmselect/cmpubadm/303/303.pdf.

Howell, William G. *Power without Persuasion: The Politics of Direct Presidential Action*. Princeton, NJ: Princeton University Press, 2003.

Hughes, Sarah. "Shonda Rhimes: Meet the Most Powerful Woman in U.S. Television." *The Independent*, September 27, 2014. http://www.independent.co.uk/arts-entertainment/tv/features/shona-rhimes-interview-meet-the-most-powerful-woman-in-us-television-9759426.html.

Hunt, Elle. "Armando Iannucci on Why He's Glad He Left *Veep*: 'I Don't Know How I'd Respond to America Now.'" *The Guardian*, May 3, 2017. https://www.the-guardian.com/books/2017/may/03/armando-iannucci-on-why-hes-glad-he-left-veep-i-dont-know-how-id-respond-to-america-now.

Jackson, Patrick Thaddeus. "Making Sense of Making Sense: Configurational Analysis and the Double Hermeneutic." In Yanow and Schwartz-Shea, *Interpretation and Method*, 264–80.

Jacobson, Louis, and Manuela Tobias. "Has Donald Trump 'Never Promoted or Encouraged Violence,' as Sarah Huckerbee Sanders said?" *Politifact*, July 5th 2017. https://www.politifact.com/truth-o-meter/statements/2017/jul/05/sarah-huckabee-sanders/has-donald-trump-never-promoted-or-encouraged-viol/

Jeffries, Stuart. "Now Is Not the Time for a Crap Opposition." *The Guardian*, October 23, 2010. https://www.theguardian.com/media/2010/oct/23/armando-ian-nucci-interview-coalition-cuts.

Jespersen, Knud J. V. *A History of Denmark*. New York: Palgrave, 2004. Kindle.

Jones, Charles O. "Richard E. Neustadt: Public Servant as Scholar." *Annual Review of Political Science* 6 (2003): 1–22.

Jones, Charles O. "Scholar-Activist as Guardian: Dick Neustadt's Presidency." In Dickinson and Neustadt, *Guardian of the Presidency*, 35–51.

Jones, Nicholas. *Sultans of Spin*. London: Gollanz, 1999.

Judis, John. *The Populist Explosion: How the Great Recession Transformed American and European Politics*. New York: Columbia Global Reports, 2016.

King, Gary. "The Methodology of Presidential Research." In *Researching the Presidency: Vital Questions, New Approaches*, edited by George C. Edwards III, John H. Kessel, and Bert A. Rockman, 387–414. Pittsburgh: University of Pittsburgh Press, 1993.

King, Gary, Robert Keohane, and Sidney Verba. *Designing Social Inquiry*. Princeton, NJ: Princeton University Press, 1994.

Kingsley, Patrick. *How to Be Danish*. New York: Atria Books, 2014. Kindle.

Kranish, Michael, and Marc Fisher. "The Insider Story of How 'The Apprentice' Rescued Donald Trump." *Fortune*, September 8, 2016. http://fortune.com/2016/09/08/donald-trump-the-apprentice-burnett.

Kristof, Nicholas. "My Shared Shame: The Media Helped Make Trump." *New York Times*, March 26, 2016. https://www.nytimes.com/2016/03/27/opinion/sunday/my-shared-shame-the-media-helped-make-trump.html.

Kuhn, Thomas. *The Structure of Scientific Revolutions*, 2nd ed. Chicago: University of Chicago Press, 1970.

Kuttner, Robert. "The Copenhagen Consensus: Reading Adam Smith in Denmark." *Foreign Affairs*, March/April 2008. https://www.foreignaffairs.com/articles/eu-rope/2008-03-01/copenhagen-consensus.

Lacan, Jacques. "The Mirror Stage as Formative of the Function of the I as Revealed in Psychoanalytic Experience," 1949. http://faculty.wiu.edu/D-Banash/eng299/LacanMirrorPhase.pdf.

Lawrence, Regina G., and W. Lance Bennett. "Rethinking Media Politics and Public Opinion: Reactions to the Clinton-Lewinsky Scandal." *Presidential Studies Quarterly* 116, no. 3 (2001): 425–46.

Leibovich, Mark. "Donald Trump Is Not Going Anywhere." *New York Times Maga-*

zine, September 29, 2015. https://www.nytimes.com/2015/10/04/magazine/donald-trump-is-not-going-anywhere.html.

Lembo, Ron. *Thinking through Television*. New York: Cambridge University Press, 2013.

Lidegaard, Bo. "Denmark's Far-Right Kingmakers." *New York Times*, June 22, 2015. https://www.nytimes.com/2015/06/22/opinion/denmarks-far-right-kingmakers.html.

Lijphart, Arend. *Patterns of Democracy: Government Forms and Performance in 38 Countries*. New Haven, CT: Yale University Press, 1999.

London School of Economics GV314 Group. "New Life at the Top: Special Advisors in British Government." Working paper, 2012. http://personal.lse.ac.uk/Pagee/Papers/GV314ParlAffairs.pdf.

Luce, Edward. *The Retreat of Western Liberalism*. New York: Atlantic Monthly Press, 2017.

Luke, Timothy, W. "Caught between Confused Critics and Careerist Co-Conspirators." In *Perestroika! The Raucous Rebellion in Political Science*, edited by Kristen Renwick Monroe, 468–88. New Haven, CT: Yale University Press, 2005.

Lynch, Michael C. *The Internet of Us*. New York: Liveright, 2016.

Lynn, Jonathan. *Comedy Rules: From the Cambridge Footlights to Yes, Minister*. London: Faber & Faber, 2011. Kindle.

Margolis, Jon. "Hart Takes on the Press, Blasts Tryst Story as False." *Chicago Tribune*, May 6, 1987.

Martin, Brett. *Difficult Men: Behind the Scenes of a Creative Revolution*. New York: Penguin, 2013.

Masket, Seth. "House of Cards Is the Worst Show about American Politics. Ever." *Washington Post*. March 8 2015. https://www.washingtonpost.com/news/monkey-cage/wp/2015/03/08/house-of-cards-is-the-worst-show-about-american-politics-ever/?utm_term=.8f9ec258f726.

Mayer, Kenneth R. *With the Stroke of a Pen: Executive Orders and Presidential Power*. Princeton, NJ: Princeton University Press, 2001.

Mayhew, David R. *Congress: The Electoral Connection*. New Haven, CT: Yale University Press, 1974.

McCann, Graham. *A Very Courageous Decision: The Inside Story of* Yes, Minister. London: Aurum Press, 2014. Kindle.

McCubbins, Mathew G., Roger G. Noll, and Barry R. Weingast. "Administrative Procedures as Instruments of Political Control." *Journal of Law, Economics, and Organization* 3, no. 2 (1987): 243–77.

McKinney, Kelsey. "The Mythmaker." *The Ringer*, January 2, 2017. https://www.theringer.com/2017/1/2/16040412/mark-burnett-donald-trump-the-celebrity-apprentice-5b1a80ad189c.

McTague, Tom, Alex Spence, and Edward-Isaac Dovere. "How David Cameron Blew It." *Politico*, June 25, 2016. https://www.politico.eu/article/how-david-cameron-lost-brexit-eu-referendum-prime-minister-campaign-remain-boris-craig-oliver-jim-messina-obama.

"Millennials across the Rich World Are Failing to Vote." *The Economist*, February 4, 2017. https://www.economist.com/news/international/21716023-democracies-are-risk-if-young-people-continue-shun-ballot-box-millennials-across.

Miller, Arthur H. "Sex, Politics, and Public Opinion: What Political Scientists Really Learned from the Clinton-Lewinsky Scandal." *PS: Political Science & Politics* 32, no. 4 (1999): 721–29.

Miller, Gary A., and Terry M. Moe. "Bureaucrats, Legislators, and the Size of Government." *American Political Science Review* 77, no. 2 (1983): 297–322.

Miller, Greg., Ellen Nakashima, and Adam Entous. "Obama's Secret Struggle to Punish Putin for Russia's Election Interference." *Washington Post*, June 23, 2017. https://www.washingtonpost.com/graphics/2017/world/national-security/obama-putin-election-hacking/?utm_term=.31173eea3f36.

Miller, Zeke J. "Obama Wishes Washington Really Was Like *House of Cards.*" *Time*, December 17, 2013. http://swampland.time.com/2013/12/17/obama-wishes-washington-was-really-like-house-of-cards.

Moe, Terry M. "Presidents, Institutions, and Theory." In *Researching the Presidency: Vital Questions, New Approaches*, edited by George C. Edwards III, John H. Kessel, and Bert A. Rockman, 337–87. Pittsburgh: University of Pittsburgh Press, 1993.

Moe, Terry M. "The Revolution in Presidential Studies." *Presidential Studies Quarterly* 39, no. 4 (2009): 701–724.

Morley, David. *Television, Audiences, and Cultural Studies*. London: Routledge, 1992.

Morley, David. "Texts, Readers, Subjects." In Hall, Hobson, Lowe, and Willis, *Culture, Media, Language*, 163–76.

Mudde, Cas, and Cristobal Rovira Kaltwasser. *Populism: A Very Short Introduction.* New York: Oxford University Press, 2017.

Neumann, Iver B. and Daniel H. Nexon, *Harry Potter and International Relations.* Lanham, MD: Rowman & Littlefield, 2006.

Neustadt, Elizabeth A. "Afterword: A Personal Reminiscence." In Dickinson and Neustadt, *Guardian of the Presidency*, 167–80.

Neustadt, Richard E. *Presidential Power and the Modern Presidents*. New York: Free Press, 1991.

"Nine Things *House of Cards* Took from Shakespeare." *Huffington Post*, February 21, 2014. http://www.huffingtonpost.com/2014/02/21/house-of-cards-shakespeare-_n_4823200.html.

Niskanen, William A. *Bureaucracy and Representative Government. Piscataway, NJ, Transaction, 1971.*

NPR, "'Hillbilly Elegy' Recalls a Childhood Where 'Poverty Was 'The Family Tradition.'" August 17th 2016. https://www.npr.org/2016/08/17/490328484/hillbilly-elegy-recalls-a-childhood-where-poverty-was-the-family-tradition

Nussbaum, Emily. "Broken News: The Artificial Intelligence of The Newsroom." *New Yorker*, June 25, 2012. http://www.newyorker.com/magazine/2012/06/25/broken-news.

Nyhan, Brendan. "Strategic Outrage: The Politics of Presidential Scandal." PhD diss., Duke University, 2009.

Oborne, Peter, and Simon Walters. *Alastair Campbell*. London: Aurum, 2004.

O'Connor, John E., and Peter C. Rollins. "Introduction." In Rollins and O'Connor, *The West Wing*, 1–16.

Oren, Ido "Political Science as History: A Reflexive Approach." In Yanow and Schwartz-Shea, *Interpretation and Method*, 215–227.

Ostergard, Uffe. "Denmark: A Big Small State—The Peasant Roots of Danish Modernity." In Campbell, Hall, and Pedersen, *National Identity and the Varieties of Capitalism*, 51–99.

Parker, Ashley. "Covering Donald Trump, Witnessing the Danger Up Close." *New York Times*, March 12, 2016. https://www.nytimes.com/2016/03/13/us/politics/covering-donald-trump-and-witnessing-the-danger-up-close.html?hp&action=click&pgtype=Homepage&clickSource=story-heading&module=first-column-region&region=top-news&WT.nav=top-news&_r=0.

Parry-Giles, Trevor, and Shawn J. Parry-Giles. *The Prime Time Presidency*: The West Wing and U.S. Nationalism. Champaign, IL: Illinois University Press, 2006.

Paskin, Willa. "Network TV Is Broken. So How Does Shonda Rhimes Keep Making Hits?" *New York Times Magazine*, May 9, 2013. http://www.nytimes.com/2013/05/12/magazine/shonda-rhimes.html.

Pedersen, Ove. K. "Corporatism and Beyond: The Negotiated Democracy." In Campbell, Hall, and Pedersen, *National Identity and the Varieties of Capitalism*, 245–70.

Perlstein, Rick. "I Thought I Understood the American Right." *New York Times Magazine*, April 11, 2017. https://www.nytimes.com/2017/04/11/magazine/i-thought-i-understood-the-american-right-trump-proved-me-wrong.html.

Podhoretz, John. "The Liberal Imagination." In Rollins and O'Connor, *The West Wing*, 222–34.

Pompper, Donnalyn. "The West Wing: White House Narratives that Journalism Cannot Tell." In Rollins and O'Connor, *The West Wing*, 17–31.

Poniewozik, James. "The New Reality of TV: All Trump, All the Time." *New York Times*, December 11, 2016. https://www.nytimes.com/2016/12/11/arts/television/the-new-reality-of-tv-all-trump-all-the-time.html.

Praino, Rodrigo, Daniel Stockemer, and Vincent G. Moscardelli. "The Lingering Effect of Scandals in Congressional Elections: Incumbents, Challengers, and Voters." *Social Science Quarterly* 94, no. 4 (2013): 1045–61.

"Pushback." *The Economist*, March 5, 2016. https://www.economist.com/books-and-arts/2016/03/05/pushback.

Quirk, Paul J. "Coping with the Politics of Scandal." *Presidential Studies Quarterly* 28, no. 4 (1998): 898–902.

Rabinow, Paul, and William M. Sullivan. "The Interpretive Turn: A Second Look." In *Interpretive Social Science: A Second Look*, edited by Paul Rabinow and William M. Sullivan, 1–32. Berkeley: University of California Press, 1987.

Rasmussen, Hjalte. "Constitutional Laxity and International High Economic Performance: Is There a Nexus?" In Campbell, Hall and Pedersen, *National Identity and the Varieties of Capitalism*, 197–244.

Renshon, Stanley A. "The Public's Response to the Clinton Scandals." *Presidential Studies Quarterly* 32, no. 1 (2002): 169–84.

Ricci, David M. *The Tragedy of Political Science: Politics, Scholarship, and Democracy*. New Haven, CT: Yale University Press, 1984.

Riker, William A. *The Theory of Political Coalitions*. New Haven, CT: Yale University Press, 1962.

Riker, William A. "The Two-Party System and Duverger's Law." *American Political Science Review* 76 (1982): 753–66.

Rollins, Peter C., and John E. O'Connor, *The West Wing: The American Presidency as Television Drama.* Syracuse, NY: Syracuse University Press, 2003.

Rose, Charlie. "Sorkin on Leaving *The West Wing,*" YouTube, https://www.youtube.com/watch?v=FEmwOQv8Pwg.

Rose, Lacey. "Julia-Louis Dreyfus Reveals Awkward Fan Letter from Hillary." *Hollywood Reporter,* April 20, 2016. http://www.hollywoodreporter.com/features/julia-louis-dreyfus-reveals-awkward-885385.

Ross, Dorothy. "The Development of the Social Sciences." In Farr and Seidelman, *Discipline and History,* 81–106.

Ruane, Abigail. E., and Patrick James. *The International Relations of Middle-Earth: Learning from "The Lord of the Rings."* Ann Arbor: University of Michigan Press, 2012.

Sabato, Larry J. *Feeding Frenzy: Attack Journalism and American Politics.* Baltimore, MD: Lanahan Publishing, 2000.

Sartori, Giovanni. *Parties and Party Systems: A Framework for Analysis.* New York: Cambridge University Press, 1976.

Scammell, Margaret. "Politics and Image: The Conceptual Value of Branding." *Journal of Political Marketing* 14, no. 1-2 (2015): 7–18.

Schlesinger, Joseph A. *Ambition and Politics: Political Careers in the United States.* Chicago: Rand McNally, 1966.

Schneider, Michael. "*House of Cards* Creator Beau Willimon on the D.C. Thriller's Second Season." *TV Guide,* February 13, 2014. http://www.tvguide.com/news/house-of-cards-season2-beau-willimon-1077696.

Schwartz, Ian. "Cokie Roberts vs. Donald Trump on Offensive Language." *Real Clear Politics,* March 9, 2016. https://www.realclearpolitics.com/video/2016/03/09/cokie_roberts_vs_donald_trump_on_offensive_language_what_about_the_children.html.

Schwartz-Shea, Peregrine, and Dvora Yanow. "'Reading' 'Methods' 'Texts': How Research Methods Texts Construct Political Science." *Political Research Quarterly* 55 (2002): 457–86.

Seidelman, Raymond. "Political Scientists, Disenchanted Realists, and Disappearing Democrats." In Farr and Seidelman, *Discipline and History,* 311–26.

Seidelman, Raymond, and Edward J. Harpham. *Disenchanted Realists: Political Science and the American Crisis, 1884–1984.* New York: SUNY Press, 1985.

Sheehy, Gail. "The Road to Bimini." *Vanity Fair,* September 1, 1987.

Shepsle, Kenneth A., and Mark S. Bonchek. *Analyzing Politics: Rationality, Behavior, and Institutions.* New York: W. W. Norton, 1997.

Smith, Judy. *Good Self, Bad Self: How to Bounce Back from a Personal Crisis.* New York: Free Press, 2013.

Sorkin, Aaron, and David Brooks. "What's Character Got to Do with It?" *The Aspen Institute.* July 1, 2015, https://www.youtube.com/watch?v=eucVNYQNGAs.

Spence, Alex. "David Cameron Unleashes Project Fear." *Politico,* February 26, 2016. http://www.politico.eu/article/david-cameron-brexit-project-fear-economy-jobs-terror-warning-britain-leaves-eu.

Stewart, Heather, and Rowena Mason. "Nigel Farage's Anti-Migrant Poster Reported to Police." *The Guardian,* June 16, 2016. https://www.theguardian.com/politics/2016/jun/16/nigel-farage-defends-ukip-breaking-point-poster-queue-of-migrants.

Stoker, Laura. "Judging Presidential Character: The Demise of Gary Hart." *Political Behavior* 15, no. 2 (1993): 193–223.

Taibbi, Matt. *Insane Clown President*. New York: Spiegel & Grau, 2017.

Taylor, Charles. "Interpretation and the Sciences of Man." In Rabinow and Sullivan, *Interpretive Social Science*, 33–81.

Taylor, Paul. *See How They Run: Electing the President in an Age of Mediaocracy*. New York: Knopf, 1990.

Russell, Helen. "The Year of Living Danishly: Uncovering the Secrets of the World's Happiest Country." London: Icon, 2016. Kindle.

US Department of Justice. "USA v. Internet Research Agency LLC et al."

Van Der Werff, Todd. "*Black Mirror* Season 3 Review." *Vox*, October 20, 2016. https://www.vox.com/culture/2016/10/20/13336942/black-mirror-season-3-review-netflix.

Van Der Werff, Todd. "How *Scandal* Became the Perfect Distillation of America's Political Nightmares." *A.V. Club*, May 6, 2013. http://www.avclub.com/article/how-iscandali-became-the-perfect-distillation-of-a-97303.

van Zoonen, Liesbet. *Entertaining the Citizen: When Politics and Popular Culture Converge*. Lanham, MD: Rowman & Littlefield, 2005.

Viner, Katharine. "How Technology Disrupted the Truth." *The Guardian*, July 12, 2016. https://www.theguardian.com/media/2016/jul/12/how-technology-disrupted-the-truth.

Waltz. Kenneth N, *Theory of International Politics*. Boston, MA: Addison-Wesley, 1979.

Ware, Alan. *Political Parties and Party Systems*. New York: Cambridge University Press, 1995.

Weldes, Jutta. "Going Cultural: *Star Trek*, State Action, and Popular Culture." Millennium: Journal of International Studies 28, no. 1 (1999).

Weldes, Jutta. "High Politics and Low Data: Globalization Discourses and Popular Culture." In Yanow and Schwartz-Shea, *Interpretation and Method*, 228–38.

Weldes, Jutta , ed. *To Seek Out New Worlds: Exploring Links between Science Fiction and World Politics*. New York: Palgrave Macmillan, 2003.

Wimpress, Chris. "*Borgen* Creator Adam Price Talks Work-Life Balance, Danish Politics, and Cameron's Mention." *Huffington Post*, February 9, 2012. http://www.huffingtonpost.co.uk/2012/02/09/borgen-creator-adam-price_n_1265437.html.

Wodskou, Chris. "*Borgen* Creator: Coalition Governments Shouldn't Be Seen as Some Kind of Weakness." *CBC News*, June 26 2015. http://www.cbc.ca/news/entertainment/borgen-creator-says-coalition-governments-shouldn-t-be-seen-as-some-kind-of-weakness-1.3129551.

Yanow, Dvora, and Peregrine Schwartz-Shea, eds. *Interpretation and Method: Empirical Research Methods and the Interpretive Turn*. New York: M. E. Sharpe, 2006.

Index

CPSIA information can be obtained
at www.ICGtesting.com
Printed in the USA
FFHW020659091019
55468089-61256FF

9 780472 054244